Consensus and Dissent

NCTE Yearbook Committee

Consensus and Dissent

Teaching English Past, Present, and Future

Editor, Marjorie N. Farmer

National Council of Teachers of English
1111 Kenyon Road, Urbana, Illinois 61801

Staff Editor: Lee Erwin

Book Design: Tom Kovacs for TGK Design

NCTE Stock Number 08342

Library of Congress Cataloging-in-Publication Data

Consensus and dissent.

Includes bibliographies.
1. English language—Study and teaching.
I. Farmer, Marjorie N., 1922– . II. National
Council of Teachers of English.
PE1065.C66 1986 428'.007 86-21324
ISBN 0-8141-0834-2

Contents

Foreword vii

Preface ix

Introduction 1

I Content: What We Teach

1. Language 15
   Harold B. Allen
2. Reading/Literature 27
   Rudine Sims
3. Written Composition: Progress and the Search for Paradigms 35
   Paul T. Bryant
4. Oral Communication 47
   Donald Rubin

II Conditions: Context for Teaching

5. The English Curriculum Today 59
   Ouida Clapp
6. Teacher Education 65
   Theodore Hipple
7. The Uses of Research 71
   Allan Glatthorn with Catherine C. Hatala and Beatrice Moore

8. Tests and the Teaching of English

Enduring Issues in Language Arts Testing 83
Rexford Brown

Minorities and Standardized Tests 88
P. A. Ramsey

9. Books and the New Technologies 95
Charles Suhor

III Change: Toward 2011

10. The Political Issues since 1960 113
Miriam T. Chaplin

11. Imperatives for the Future 127
James R. Squire

12. NCTE Presidents: Priorities for the Future 133
Nancy S. McHugh, Sheila Fitzgerald, Richard Lloyd-Jones, and Stephen N. Tchudi

The View from Headquarters 143
John C. Maxwell

Afterword 145

Contributors 149

Foreword

This first NCTE yearbook is being published in conjunction with the Diamond Jubilee of the National Council of Teachers of English. From the beginning, the Yearbook Committee thought that this first volume should focus on issues which have repeatedly surfaced in the Council's deliberations, issues that are also likely to be of particular concern in the immediate future.

We on the committee continually found ourselves thinking in terms of a series of dichotomies that have informed Council debates through the years, e.g., freedom and discipline, tradition and reform, excellence in education and equity in education, theory and practice, the common curriculum and individual differences, English teaching as a profession and English teaching as a craft, "basic skills" and "essentials of education," process and product, and more. The list seems endless. What these dichotomies reflect is a profession defining itself in a rhythm of consensus and dissent. We were particularly concerned with how the classroom teacher deals with these conflicting pressures—or, as one committee member said, with the teacher "caught between dichotomies."

Because Marjorie Farmer has such a sensitive ear for the voices heard in our profession, we were delighted that she consented to edit this volume. Her knowledge of the history of the Council and her continuing concern for the classroom teacher prepared her to focus on recurring issues important to the profession and to attract authors who speak with authority and who represent the broad spectrum of the profession of English.

Though the issues discussed in this volume have been identified from a historical perspective, these essays focus primarily on the present and the future. Though they are grounded in theory and research, they address problems of the teacher as practitioner and decision maker. Though they are organized around reasonably discrete aspects of our work, they continually revert to the same themes. Though the voices of the authors differ, they speak in the same idiom. They bear a family resemblance.

We think that these essays both describe and demonstrate the continuing dialogue that has made the Council's history so exciting. We hope that they impel responses that will continue and enhance that dialogue.

Ben F. Nelms, Chair
NCTE Yearbook Committee

Preface

"You shall proclaim release throughout the land for all its inhabitants.
It shall be a jubilee for you . . ." (Leviticus 25:10)

The jubilee tradition we are celebrating in this yearbook is marked by the same creative tension that shapes our history as a community of English teachers. Jubilee calls us to liberation, to homecoming, to self-knowledge. But it is a freedom defined by a precisely detailed set of laws. We come home to a land that we can never really possess; we are tenants, holding it in trust. And when we come to know ourselves, we see the faces of strangers in our own. It is this wholeness, this life-giving balance of essential opposites, that we celebrate.

Freedom or discipline, basic skills or humanities, academic content or communication competencies, process or product: what is English? How do we teach it best? How can we care so much about our work and fail so many of our students? How do we reach sometimes beyond the limits of our knowledge and teach so amazingly well? What firm yet fragile consensus governs our ordinary, everyday teaching? Every brief certainty contains its inevitable questions; we teach in the space between our dichotomies; we agree on what we're doing in the pauses between our disagreements. This is the life-giving dialectic of our work. This is what we celebrate in this yearbook.

The essays in this collection are intended to invite you—teacher, student, friend, critic—to come into our jubilee dialogue. The English language and its literature set the boundaries of our intellectual home; dialogue is the jubilee that releases the written word into living communication. Each essay is a personal statement, deeply rooted in familiarity with our common history and interpreted through a particular and unique life experience. Each essayist has had the challenge of the penetrating criticism of highly interactive readers; each welcomes you into the continuing conversation. In each paper you may hear your own voice—or the voice of a friend or stranger. You may wish to make your own response or your own statement, perhaps using the Council's conferences and publications, affiliate workshops, your own faculty meetings or lecture halls—or any of a number of responsive audiences—as your forum. We hope you will want to hear what each essayist has said, and that it will matter to you that you did so.

The editor has been a grateful listener and participant in the life of this yearbook. Its imperfections are signs chiefly of her limitations. Where you find it, however briefly, true and brilliant with the diamond clarity of self-knowledge—telling us who we are and what our teaching is and what it is becoming—this is testimony to the wisdom and the perseverance of the writers and editorial advisers.

The vitality of the dialogue requires your voice as well. Welcome to the conversation!

Marjorie N. Farmer

Introduction

In Thornton Wilder's "The Long Christmas Dinner," several generations of the same family drift in and out of the dining room of the family home over a period of ninety years, always talking. The costumes change, the names change, the words change, but the themes of their conversation remain much the same. In some ways the history of the National Council of Teachers of English has been like a long Thanksgiving dinner. The faces change, the names change, the topics change, but the themes remain much the same. (No doubt this is one of the reasons that, year after year, so many Council members have insisted on hearing members of the same publishing family—father and son—deliver the same words of the same speech, the text of which has been provided, like the feast, by the "sponsor who shall remain nameless.")

In preparing this book on the occasion of the NCTE Diamond Jubilee, we have often referred to the Council's debates through the years, its continuing dialogue, its discussions and deliberations. Indeed, Council members have debated one another, have deliberated and discussed. At times, various ones of its members have declaimed, denounced, and decried. But, all in all, the exchanges have been more in the nature of a long, vigorous, but friendly conversation. As Allan Glatthorn and his colleagues remind us in their essay on the uses of research, citing Margret Buchmann, "In conversation, ideas . . . collide and mingle with one another and are diluted and complicated in the process."

Through the years, the Council has often been divided by specific, controversial issues. Often, too, like a rowdy family we have been united by threats from external sources. But more often than not the thrust of our talk—in our journals, our conventions, our committees, our documents and correspondence—has been not confrontational but conversational. Conversation, again according to Buchmann, "respects great differences and ranges easily over different provinces of meaning." One purpose of this volume has been to eavesdrop on certain episodes in this conversation and to add to it by recapitulating and extrapolating its major themes.

What voices from the past speak to our present concerns? What sense of collective identity do they provide for this "family of English teachers," as

Executive Director John Maxwell calls us? More important, what basis do they provide for our decision making in the next quarter of a century?

The authors of the essays in this volume enter the history of our profession at interestingly different points. Harold Allen, one of our true patresfamilias, quite naturally begins his account of changes in the study of the English language at about the time of the founding of the Council and follows the course of its debates (in most of which he has at one time or another played an active role) through seventy-five years, tracing our internal squabbles from their roots to their resolution. Don Rubin, for other obvious reasons, dates the beginnings of certain tensions about the teaching of oral communication back to Aristotle's argument with the Sophists in ancient Greece. Rudine Sims begins with the act requiring the establishment of schools and the promotion of literacy in seventeenth-century Massachusetts, and Paul Bryant with early instruction in rhetoric at Harvard. Ted Hipple, with tongue only slightly in cheek, begins with cave dwellers. Miriam Chaplin marks the beginning of our current era of change and challenge with such legislative mandates as the Civil Rights Act of 1964 and PL 94–142 eleven years later. Charles Suhor recalls the expanding interest in media in the late sixties, when articles with titles like "Hook Up, Plug In, Connect" held our attention.

Indeed, the historical perspective provided in most of the chapters of this volume is limited to that period of Council history in which the current generation of our family has taken part—the last twenty-five years or so. One way to sample the ideas in a book and to test for consensus among various sections is to play the indexing game. What names, titles, topics show up in the index most often? In most chapters of the book? It might be expected that the persons, agencies, and documents that have most influenced all aspects of our recent history and that might be most significant in envisioning future directions would be mentioned frequently by the authors of these essays—either approvingly or pejoratively. In fact, one is hardly surprised to find many names from outside our immediate professional family mentioned prominently, from Mortimer Adler to Marshall McLuhan, from Carl Rogers to Mel and Norma Gabler, nor to find the leading lights to be Jean Piaget and Jerome Bruner and John Goodlad. Within the family those most often cited—always approvingly—are James Moffett, James Britton, Janet Emig, and Mina Shaughnessy. Among topics, transformational/generative grammar and writing across the curriculum head the list, the latter with a great deal more enthusiasm than the former. The College Entrance Examination Board's Commission on English, with its report *Freedom and Discipline in English,* the National Assessment of Education Progress, and the NCTE Commission on Curriculum, with three reports in about as many decades, all receive some comment. But if you put any credence in this indexing game at all, it is clear that the only agency in our recent history to be cited in almost every chapter no matter what the topic—about three times as often as any other—is the Anglo-American Seminar on the Teaching of English in 1966, the Dartmouth Seminar. Whether the topic be oral language or literature, technology or curriculum, social equality or academic excellence, Dartmouth and our British cousins who joined us there seem to have exerted their influence. What led up to Dartmouth? What has proceeded from it? The answers to those questions will provide a framework for reading the essays in this yearbook. Rarely has an event enlivened Council conversation to the degree that the deliberations of this small conclave did. Rarely has a movement within the Council produced the level of intellectual inquiry and passionate commitment that it did. It did not, however, usher in an era of national consensus nor become the foundation for an immediate movement toward national reform in English.

The last time there was a national agenda for teachers of English—a platform upon which the profession was united—was in the late fifties or early sixties, at the time of the preparation and publication of *The National Interest and the Teaching of English* in 1961. This document embodied the response of the Council and other associations to the post-Sputnik emphasis on mathematics and science, the call for academic rigor in schools and in teacher education, and the case for provision of federal funds for education "for the national defense." Ironically, all the most visible achievements of that era—NDEA summer institutes in teacher education, Project English centers for curriculum development, and a loose network of research efforts under the auspices of the Cooperative Research Program of the U.S. Office of Education—have since been abandoned and in certain cases repudiated. The NDEA institutes often turned out to be isolated one-shot academic exercises dominated by university models of curriculum and instruction and divorced from the realities of many classrooms, especially those populated by students of lesser ability, lower socioeconomic status, or modest levels of motivation. Likewise, the Project English centers for the most part produced materials arranged in the then-familiar triad—linguistics, literary analysis, and rhetoric—which satisfied our collective yen for symmetry and logical sequence more than they met the interests, needs, and abilities of many of our students. The research model that held sway, and for the first time brought experimental behaviorists and classical humanists into league with each other, was the scientific/experimental design. Just a cursory review of the last decade of our journal *Research in the Teaching of English* suggests that this model has given way to various case studies, discourse analyses, and naturalistic or ethnographic methods of describing students, their reading, and their writing. Even the more broadly influential studies of teacher effectiveness and school effectiveness have relied on large-N correlational studies rather than rigorous experimental designs for most of their conclusions.

Summer institutes on the NDEA model, curriculum projects patterned after Project English, and the scientific/experimental studies of the Cooperative Research Program have all but disappeared from our professional landscape in English. So much for the influence and effectiveness of our national agenda. Before it was repudiated, however, it was abandoned. The social climate changed. The political winds blew cold. Almost overnight, funds for such programs of teacher education, curriculum development, and cooperative research in English not only dwindled, but virtually disappeared. Perhaps in the years of plenty funds were spent unwisely, maybe even squandered. No Joseph prepared us for the years of famine. But more damning than the failure of funds was the failure of will. The national consensus that had prevailed in the early sixties was undermined and ultimately fragmented in the turmoil of the late sixties. Among English teachers the national agenda gave way to a national crisis of conscience; optimism gave way to uncertainty. The euphoria of the halcyon years was replaced by an excess of guilt at the end of the decade. English teachers not only shared the blame for oppressing minorities, neglecting the disadvantaged, ignoring the less able, endangering the psychic health of the young, and repressing their own best instincts, but also accepted responsibility for contributing to the linguistic and intellectual climate that made Watts, Vietnam, and Watergate possible, maybe even inevitable. Teaching, we were told, should be a subversive activity. Speakers who commanded our attention at national conventions pleaded for relevance, soft revolutions, and student-centered curricula. The impetus for change may have been largely external—social, political, economic—but the origin of the self-doubt that became self-condemnation was also internal, implicit in what was emerging as a clearer understanding of the language and learning of the young. The gurus of the movement—sometimes maybe against their will—were Ken Macrorie, Ken Goodman, and James Moffett. But the super-guru was a modest scholar from England, James Britton. The intellectual basis for the awakened national conscience among American English teachers was a British import, a modest retreat that brought together Anglo-American teachers of English at Dartmouth in the summer of 1966. The chapter titles of one report on the conference indicate some of its major emphases: democracy in the classroom, the development of the child, "good English" (the quotation marks are significant), the uses of literature, writing and talking, creativity and drama, mass media and myth, and issues of responsibility. What is missing in the list is almost as significant as what appears: the discipline of English, linguistics in the classroom, critical approaches to literature, ancient and modern rhetoric, scope and sequence in the English curriculum—all topics that had been dear to the heart of Project English and other curriculum reformers in the early sixties.

But the imperatives of Dartmouth were not immediately enacted in American classrooms. The social and political climate of the post-Sputnik era had fostered a unity of will that had been reflected in the national agenda for English teachers. When this will was fragmented by racial unrest, war protests, and political corruption, a period of disunity and withdrawal followed. We never utterly abandoned the hopes wrapped up in our national agenda nor the ideals engendered by our national conscience. But, by 1973, our profession appeared to be floundering. The job market had plummeted, funding for research and development had been drastically curtailed, our graduate programs were dwindling, our most basic professional values were under attack, our morale was low, and our will and energy were undermined by self-doubt—we were divided within and threatened without. We had become a large, unhappy family, ill at ease among ourselves. The public perception of our effectiveness may have reached its nadir in December 1975 with the publication of the *Newsweek* cover story "Why Johnny Can't Write," which began simply, "If your children are attending college, the chances are that when they graduate they will be unable to write ordinary, expository English. . . ." Our patrons were demanding that we go "back to the basics," and sometimes we attempted to pacify them.

However, English teachers as a group could never—personally or professionally—adapt to the narrow schemes of an industrial management complex. Behavioral objectives, cost effectiveness, accountability, instructional management, performance-based teacher evaluation, management by objectives—even the language of this movement stuck in our craws. The vision of teaching which the terms promulgated never could be incorporated into our professional self-image, which had emerged slowly through half a century and then had been shaped, tried, and melted down in the cauldron of the sixties. Administrators, forced by law to evaluate teachers and unwilling or unable to do so, promoted the use of templates for lesson planning that resembled instructions for a sales pitch (one version was called the Super-7 Plus 3). What we were being offered was fragmentation, a mechanical and cynical scheme for preserving order and the status quo. What we had envisioned was wholeness. Granted, within one decade we had constructed two very different visions of wholeness. In the era of consensus our national agenda had imagined wholeness as a triangle, a logical, coherent pattern with structure, system, sequence, discipline, and a hierarchy of interrelated values. In the era of dissent, our national conscience had imagined wholeness as a circle, each arc organically related to the other, with interactive growth, empathy, self-determination, and intrinsic motivation at its center. Both of our most recent visions maintained a picture of linguistic and pedagogical wholeness, freedom and discipline for learners to learn and teachers to teach. The M & M's of the seventies—measurement and management—threatened both.

At the height of the public controversy, Margaret Early in her presidential address issued a quiet but firm call to renewal—not a flashy organizational renewal, but the sort of day-to-day renewal that good teachers have always required and had to provide for themselves (*English Journal* 36 [Nov. 1974]: 10–13): "Anew each day—or at least each year—we have to determine what is English for these students, for this one; for these teachers, for this particular one, for me." Her words struck the note for another new and exciting era for our professional family. What seems finally to have emerged in the last decade in our country, perhaps beginning when we watched the tall ships sail out of New York Harbor on July 4, 1976, is being called by social critics a national reconciliation. In the teaching of English it might more appropriately be called a national compromise—or, if that word has taken on too pejorative a tone, a new realism. It pays homage to the basic skills movement by emphasizing reading and writing and critical thinking. It has rediscovered some of the elements of the Project English triad, which had been too quickly abandoned in the sixties: generative rhetoric with its emphasis on the composing process, modern literary criticism with its growing interest in readers' response, and descriptive linguistics, especially its insights into language variation, language learning, sentence style, and the sociopsychological dimensions of language. It adapted both the conclusions and the method of the Dartmouth Seminar, that is, a small group of dedicated teachers working together for some length of time in a quiet retreat.

This new realism or national compromise in English is not merely an eclectic approach, merging conflicting elements, or a compromise in the sense of a hedging of principle. It shows promise of being what Margaret Early surely envisioned—a national renewal on a personal level. At its center is a renewed respect for teachers and teaching. If the national agenda gave too much emphasis to our subject in the abstract, and the period of national conscience too much attention to the surface interests of our students, the new realism may have found the natural balance in the teacher, for it is the classroom teacher who mediates between subject and students every day.

The essays in this book reflect this balance. The defining characteristics of this new movement, if it is indeed a movement, and thus the recurring themes in this yearbook, are (1) a recognition of the professionalism of teachers, (2) a vision of the integrity of our discipline, and (3) the reconciliation of theory, research, and practice in the classroom.

In teacher education and staff development, this renewal is exemplified most prominently by the Bay Area Writing Project and its emulators (BAWP was one of the few programs to be mentioned favorably in the notorious *Newsweek* article). It is also seen in the loose national network of teacher support groups, called by various ingenious acronyms, the most frequently used one being TAWL (Teachers Applying Whole Language), and in a host of ad hoc organizations, assemblies, retreats, and consortia that have sprung up on the margins of NCTE, or in the interspaces between the MLA and NCTE or IRA and NCTE, e.g., WPA (Writing Program Administrators), CELT (Center for Expansion of Language and Thinking), the Writing Centers Association, the Children's Literature Association, and the like. These are loosely organized support groups which exist in networks with one another and coexist quite peacefully with the older, more traditional organizations. They grew up as a kind of reality therapy and serve much the same function that was envisioned for teacher centers earlier. They address the questions, What can teachers learn from one another? What can beginning teachers or insecure teachers learn from experienced teachers who have survived, not only survived but succeeded? What can teachers learn from their own classrooms? from their colleagues' experiences? their explanations? their demonstrations? Interestingly enough, teachers thus respected and invited into a collegial relationship with one another open themselves sometimes enthusiastically, sometimes reluctantly, but almost always gratefully to accommodation, change, risk, and experimentation. In other words, the theory and research which they might previously have shunned as being hostile or unrealistic in their settings they are willing to consider. More important, on the basis of their collective experience they contribute insights and speculations to a growing body of theory, and data and analyses of data to a growing body of classroom-based research. Almost invariably these groups have broken down professional barriers: between elementary and secondary teaching, reading and writing, process and product, popular or folk traditions and belletristic traditions, self-expression and communication, and so on. Thus they restore, or maybe even invent, the integration of the language arts, the integrity of our discipline.

In research, the national renewal in English has preferred a new methodology more consistent with its character. The national agenda had insisted on the scientific/experimental model, its rigorous design uniting the behavioral psychologists and the subject-matter specialists. Out of the era of our national conscience came a distrust for generalization and impersonal conclusions about teaching and learning. We turned more to the study of our students—their writing processes, their linguistic growth, their characteristic responses to literature, their reading miscues, their errors and expectations. This basic research enlightened us about our students and their comprehension of our subject, but only indirectly provided bases for decision-making in the classroom. With the new realism we turn with renewed interest to our classrooms as research laboratories. Still suspicious of generalization and acontextual conclusions, we nevertheless seek direction, reliable solutions to problems, and applicable teaching strategies. Thus we turn more and more to ethnographic and naturalistic methods and to action research. Analysis and rational conclusions are both undergirded *and* undercut by anecdote, exempla, and exception.

The contribution of the national renewal to curriculum development has been less conspicuous. It is not so much that curriculum planning is anathema to the new realism but that the reality from which it sprang has taught us that new textbooks, new curriculum guides, new lists of objectives, and new tests of achievement are unlikely to bring about change. Classroom strategies and classroom language have been the focus of both teacher education and research. Reports of self-generated curricula have been narrative rather than regulatory, episodic rather than comprehensive, and personal rather than institutional. Curriculum development, as a matter of fact, has been almost an underground activity, accommodating itself to whatever overt curricular structures it inherits from the system but adapting and infiltrating on its own terms. Thus far, it has been more successful in writing than in reading, where the complicated question of what our children will read has not been answered very well. We vacillate between "whatever they want to read" or "whatever we have available" and "whatever their parents read " or "whatever they need to succeed." Problems of censorship, copyright, pressures on publishers, declining support for libraries, increasing media distraction, and emphasis on the utilitarian aims of education have combined to render us timid in curriculum reform, especially in literature and reading.

The real message regarding curriculum development, however, is that method and material are organically related, that the act of teaching must reflect the nature of learning, that common learning and individual choice are not inconsistent, and that language processes transcend the traditional boundaries of our discipline. Thus writing across the curriculum, reading across the curriculum, and the reading-writing connection are among the ways in which the curriculum has responded to the new realism.

The recurring themes in the first two sections of this yearbook are that what we teach determines how we teach and that how we teach affects what is taught and learned. The dichotomy between subject and method, between curriculum and instruction, is a false dichotomy. One cannot read Harold Allen's essay on the study of language without wondering whether the findings of descriptive research can be taught and learned prescriptively. Or Rudine Sims's essay, without wondering whether the study of reading and literature can be separated in schools without falsifying both and confusing students. Or Paul Bryant, without agreeing that writing and reading may in the fullest sense define humanity and, on a practical level, connect rhetoric and literary criticism, "reuniting those sometimes schizophrenic sides of so many college English departments." Or Donald Rubin's essay, without wondering whether oral and interpersonal communication can be excluded from a curriculum or ignored in a classroom that proceeds largely by oral discussion and personal interaction.

Thus Rubin strikes the keynote for the first two sections of the yearbook, the organic relationship of subject and method: "We will need to think about our students' language and interaction as the text from which we teach." Part 1 simply emphasizes the content of English, what we teach; part 2 shifts the focus a bit toward the profession of English, the conditions within which we teach. Ouida Clapp reiterates and generalizes Rubin's call for balance and organic harmony within the English curriculum. Commenting on three disparate curriculum models described in a recent NCTE publication, she concludes that, in recent manifestations, they are not so disparate: "Operating in each teaching-learning mode is a centering sense . . . that recognizes the need for attention to both cognitive and affective development, the desirability of respect for tradition as well as reform, and . . . the fact that parts belong to wholes." It is clear from the essays in part 2 that the collective influence of classroom teachers is needed to reform and renew the English curriculum, teacher education, educational research, and testing and evaluation. Theodore Hipple points to the key role of practicing teachers when he worries about our "uncertain straddling" between educating teachers for schools that are and educating them for schools that ought to be. Master teachers must provide the laboratories in which apprentices begin their induction into the profession. According to Glatthorn and his colleagues, they also provide our research laboratories: instead of viewing the classroom as a place where research findings are applied, the classroom should become " 'the ground for inquiry,' the focus of research" and classroom teachers must become full partners in the enterprise.

Even the effects of testing, a common concern among these writers, must be reconciled with the aims of teaching. If minimum competency tests tend to narrow what is taught, Rexford Brown contends, "It is equally sensible to believe that more imaginative and comprehensive evaluations—whether teacher-made or commercial—might broaden or deepen the curriculum or change the ways we teach English over the next seventy-five years." He garners support from an unexpected source: Rubin maintains that when assessments of students' speaking and listening are "carefully prepared to reflect the rhetorical aims of communication education . . . they can indeed serve as the impetus for positive innovations." P. A. Ramsey also is optimistic, especially about the teacher's role in influencing this branch of the educational establishment. He believes it is within the collective power of educators to improve testing. "When you, the people who use the tests, unite and speak, your voice is heard."

Charles Suhor is not altogether sanguine about our ability to look ahead, though he, too, holds out some hope that teachers may change the conditions under which we teach. Though he admits that most predictions in the social sciences are simply errors made in advance, he continues, "I believe that the only prophecies worth making . . . are those that are self-fulfilling by reason of our determination to make them come true." Perhaps we should have taken more literally the title of Edmund Farrell's monograph a few years ago: *Deciding the Future.*

Thus part 3 of this volume looks to the future and envisions teachers as active agents of change. In recent years, according to Miriam Chaplin, teachers have had to adjust to sweeping changes imposed by legislation and public policy. In the social and political arenas, she maintains, teachers must also exercise their professional expertise and assume responsibility for their own destinies. They must use peripheral vision to look about them and extended vision to look ahead. It is the hope of the Yearbook Committee that yearbooks like this one can contribute to both kinds of vision. The last two pieces in this present volume abandon reportorial objectivity in favor of James Squire's modest proposal and his not-so-new imperatives and in favor of the continued dialogue among Council leaders recorded in the final chapter. The sprawling family of English teachers has not usually functioned very well as a militant clan. It is clear, however, that its leaders have fashioned banners under which it might willingly march.

What does all this say to the classroom teacher? The Yearbook Committee worried about that question early, regularly, and seriously from the time that it decided that the first NCTE yearbook should bear a historical theme. We reasoned, however, that the essays presented here articulate insights on two of the three levels that Glatthorn (following Connelly and Elbaz) calls teachers' *personal practical knowledge.* They do not, of course, attempt to present *rules of practice;* this is not the proper forum for that level of specificity, though that may be the province of successive yearbooks. They do include *practical principles* (e.g., Sims's "create literate environments in which students and teachers read, write, and talk to each other daily about issues of concern to them and to the society at large"), and they include authentic *images* (Brown's comparison of standardized test scores to the Dow-Jones average or Chaplin's vision that the teachers' task is "to gaze on the landscape of their profession and find the hills to build on and the hillocks to level out.") In most instances, these principles and images are not so much addressed to poor or insecure teachers as they are derived from the experience of good teachers.

We were very much aware of teachers' dilemmas, not just instructional and curricular dilemmas but also those involved in the "dailiness" of the teaching life. We were aware of the problems articulated by Stuart Palonsky in his book *900 Shows a Year: A Look at Teaching from a Teacher's Side of the Desk,* especially in the section he calls "Feeling Unsupported and Vulnerable":

> The loneliness of teaching is one of its most widely recognized characteristics. Teachers spend most of their working lives away from colleagues, supervisors, administrators, or other adults.
>
> Teachers have no mechanisms to resolve conflicts over curriculum or teaching styles, so they avoid them.
>
> Bells define teachers' working days: Meet the students at the door; make sure they get to class on time; start teaching when the bell rings; don't stop teaching until you hear another bell; never, never dismiss the students before the bell.
>
> Unless teachers pursue graduate courses on their own time, they have only chance encounters with their academic discipline and the field of education.
>
> Administrators seem as concerned with order as they are with instruction. It is hard to determine if the students are learning anything; it is easier to tell if they have their feet on the library tables.
>
> Administrators may have been locked into their roles as apologists for the school, and they are forced to ignore substantive school problems because they have to project the image that the school is functioning safely, efficiently, and without conflict or dissent.
>
> Teachers believe that the school treats them poorly. Classes are routinely interrupted; conferences with parents are scheduled without consultation; teachers cannot on their own leave the building during the school day.
>
> When you teach 900 classes of adolescents a year, there are bound to be problems.
>
> (Adapted from Palonsky [New York: Random House, 1986], 175–78)

It is precisely to these needs of "this family of English teachers" that the National Council of Teachers of English has so regularly and effectively ministered—the need for camaraderie and collegiality, for self-determination and self-criticism, for respect and recognition, for intellectual stimulation and professional exchange. John Maxwell writes, "We must perceive the Council as a continuing forum for the exploration of possible truths about the art and science of teaching English." And thus we return once again to dichotomies: the tentativeness of *exploration,* the exactness of *truths*; art and science; freedom and discipline. Stephen Tchudi, who first conceived this NCTE yearbook series, quite appropriately gives voice to a last and important dilemma facing the Council at the time of its Diamond Jubilee: that is, the nature of the Council itself, now that the nuclear family of 1911 has become an extended family, even a clan, in 1986. "We have to face the fact that the National Council of Teachers of English has become a bureaucracy. It is a humanistic bureaucracy as opposed to a materialistic one, but it is a bureaucracy nonetheless. . . . We sometimes rejoice in the healthy diversity of NCTE and in its capability of tolerating divergent points of view. At the same time, the Council has lost some of the focus it had during its early years." An open forum? or a self-sustaining bureaucracy? Diversity of views? or unity of focus? As in so many other areas, the *teachers of English* who make up this *national council* must choose their own future.

In any case, the questions should provide several more lively hours of table conversation at our long Thanksgiving dinner. During the past twenty-five years, that conversation has focused on the failure of a national agenda, a national crisis of conscience, and the national threat of an industrial management model of teaching. It has celebrated a national renewal of energy and vision, based on heightened professionalism among classroom teachers and their uncompromising sense of realism about the teaching of English. The conversation shows no sign of lagging or of lapsing into silence or gibberish. Let the talk go on.

Ben F. Nelms
Marjorie N. Farmer

I Content: What We Teach

1 Language

Harold B. Allen

In the late 1960s about eighteen thousand elementary and secondary school teachers of English and the language arts attended 440 NDEA institutes throughout the nation, within the context of the institutes' concept—earlier offered by the College Entrance Examination Board and bolstered in the Basic Issues Conferences of 1958—that English is a tripod composed of literature, composition, and language.

It may be doubted whether many of those teachers rejected that now-familiar concept on the really obvious ground that the three legs of this postulated tripod are not comparable entities. After all, there would be no English literature without the English language. There would be no English composition without the English language. But the existence of the English language does not depend upon the existence of either literature or the discipline of English composition. Rather, it is the other way around: literature and composition rest upon the monolithic base of the language itself. There is no tripod. It can hardly be a non sequitur, then, to insist that teachers of English and their students should be provided with sound information about the English language and, indeed, about the nature of language itself.

The need for such sound information has surfaced many times in the life of the National Council of Teachers of English, as certain language issues and concerns have given rise to different, sometimes sharply contrasting, points of view. Let me roughly alphabetize some of the principal debates: bidialectalism and bilingualism; dictionary use; grammar (variously considered as what grammar to teach, how grammar should be taught, and what purpose is served by the teaching of grammar); linguistics as subject matter and linguistics as applied to such fields as reading, spelling, composition, and literary criticism; regional variation; teacher training in the English language; unethical use of language; usage and its recent perspective in the field of social dialectology; and vocabulary acquisition and growth.

It is true that in its first seventy-five years the Council never quite lost sight of the language that had given it its name. The role of the language in early years of Council life was, however, often ambiguous if not marginal, the vision sometimes dim and myopic, and concern with preparing teachers to provide that sound information usually either minimal or nonexistent.

Yet during those first decades ample information about the English language was available to all Council leaders had they only sought it. Few did. From the early development of descriptive linguistics in the nineteenth century, there already had emerged the great English grammars of Maetzner, Kruisinga, Poutsma, Sonnenschein, and Sweet, as well as the first books by Otto Jespersen. Hermann Paul's *Principles of the History of Language* had been translated into English in 1889. Leon Kellner's *Historical Outlines of English Syntax* was published in 1892, Oliver Emerson's *History of the English Language* in 1894, George Philip Krapp's *Modern English: Its Growth and Present Use* in 1909, and Leonard Bloomfield's *Introduction to the Study of Language* in 1914. With respect to usage, Thomas R. Lounsbury of Yale University had produced *The Standard of Usage in English* in 1908, following his *Standard of Pronunciation in English* of 1904. J. Lesslie Hall's evidential *English Usage* appeared in 1917.

Although some of the kind of information these scholarly works contained was reflected from time to time in a few Council convention papers and journal articles, only with respect to usage was there noticeable impact upon the Council itself or the profession as a whole for nearly half a century. It remained for social and political developments and a new and revolutionary linguistic theory to expand concern with language matters and to draw upon the expanding body of linguistic theory and knowledge.

Why was there such minimal impact? We might look to a seemingly innate resistance by many teachers to any language statement or linguistic fact that disturbed their implicit and uncritical acceptance of the status quo. If schoolteachers in general have been characterized as a conservative social force, then, linguistically, English teachers on all levels fully justified that allegation. Any suggested departure from the status quo brought a knee-jerk reaction among the great majority. Instant polarity developed. The guardians of "the purity of the language" rushed to the barricades. Such reaction generally was strongest in the elementary field, but secondary school English teachers were often just as reluctant to forsake their vested interest in what they were daily teaching; among college teachers likewise there were those who were hesitant to depart from Alexander Pope's caveat against innovation. To follow the succession of these polarities in the life of the Council leads us to appreciate the diverse and lively interest in recent specific issues.

Two distinct polarities appeared in the Council's first decades. One was the polarity between language statements derived from the eighteenth-century Procrustean adaptations of Latin grammar to the English language and statements based upon observation of the actual practice of English language users. The other polarity was that between prescriptive Latinate rules for the student to apply in both speech and writing and usage rules applying the statements describing *actual* language practice. The ambiguity rests in the fact that traditional grammar itself is essentially a body of usage rules. For the teacher, *grammar* and *usage* were synonymous terms. A major case study by Charles C. Fries thoroughly exemplified this problem with respect to the rules prescribing and those describing the so-called future tense, his "expression of the future" (in *The Teaching of the English Language,* 1927), although it was years before his research modified the traditional rules of the textbooks.

Grammatical Nomenclature

Over the subordinate issue of nomenclature the confusion was evident even as the Council was being born. The first question raised in the new Council was "When we teach grammar, what names shall we use?" At the founding convention in 1911 perceptive Edwin Lewis of Chicago's Lewis Institute said, "It is not necessary for our school grammars to carry a mass of unscientific, factitious, make-believe phraseology, the residue of an obsolete psychology," and he was echoed by C. N. Rourke of Milwaukee, who said, "At the present time, in twenty-five English texts there are ten different names for the use of *good* in the sentence *He is good* and eighteen different names for the use of *red* in the sentence *He painted the barn red.*" Like all good Americans the participants in the discussion promptly formed a committee to consider the terminological confusion. Although two years later the committee did succeed in agreeing upon a uniform nomenclature for textbooks and classroom use, teachers with a lifelong attachment to *predicate noun* resolutely refused to accept *subject complement,* and those who deeply cherished *subject complement* were equally adamant in rejecting *predicate noun.* The committee report died aborning.

Then in 1958 the infusion of new terms from structural grammar led to a rebirth of the issue and the consequent formation of a new committee on grammatical terminology. The committee held two meetings of textbook writers and authors, one at the NCTE convention and one at the Modern Language Association convention. Inability of the participants to agree left intact the amorphous body of grammatical terms, a body soon to be further diversified in a few textbooks by authors who had accepted transformational grammar, along with *its* version of, for example, the predicate nominative, as the NP in the rewriting of the VP component of NP + VP when the V is a form of *be.*

But the validity of traditional school grammar itself had rarely been seriously questioned during those early years. True, some doubts had been expressed about methods of teaching it, since evidence already indicated that it was not accomplishing the stated purpose of improving students' control of so-called correct English. At the 1912 convention L. R. Brown of Cleveland opined that the teaching of grammar needed "adjustments," an opinion shared by two speakers who dared to propose that some parts of it could safely be eliminated. But they were not advocating a different grammar. They simply sought to break up the solid mass of 150-year-old rules by teaching and drilling a particular rule when its frequent violation seemed to demand immediate remediation. Thus began what was called "functional grammar," bits and pieces of the traditional corpus administered widely for some two decades like homeopathic pills for specific ailments. One result was that students could never acquire any concept of the language as a coherent and complex system, even in such superficial terms as had been provided by the intermittently popular Reed and Kellogg diagramming of 1885. Grammar must have been an incomprehensible mess for students.

Nevertheless an early hint of the rejection of the rigidity of school grammar rules appeared in 1917 in an *English Journal* article by the Council's first president, Fred Newton Scott of the University of Michigan. American English expressions, he wrote, are as admissible as those of British English, and he offered the heretical opinion that there is nothing wrong with the colloquial forms of the language. In 1919 a stronger and more direct attack was a maverick article by Ella Heaton Pope, who wanted linguistics taught in high school and college, a proposition so bizarre that she felt compelled to define linguistics for her readers. Yet, although a year later W. P. Reeves amplified the views of Scott and Pope, polarity was maintained by an official Council committee that same year, whose report doggedly declared that a thorough understanding of grammar, i.e., Latinate grammar, was necessary "to the mastery of the sentence and for the correction of certain errors in accepted grammatical usage." But the defenders of the status quo must have felt besieged when in 1924 one of Scott's former graduate students, Charles C. Fries, also to become a Council president, collected a panel of six outstanding language scholars to answer three questions: 1. What should the English teacher know about the English language? 2. Do the usual college courses in Old English, historical grammar, and Chaucer give prospective English teachers an adequate introduction to the language? 3. Has linguistic scholarship any practical help to offer in the problem of teaching correct English? Needless to say, their answers did not please the traditionalists.

From the distant perspective of sixty years, Fries's early leadership in thus enlisting the support of these six scholars was indeed portentous. Himself both scholar and speaker, Fries was already beginning a distinguished career in the Council, one marked by insistence upon continued research in the living language, upon providing teachers with knowledge of the grammar of the language in terms of its syntax as well as of its obvious paradigms, and upon making that grammar the basis of the language concepts and attitudes to be taught in the schools.

Development of the Resolution on Language Training

During the next three years, 1925 through 1927, Fries followed through by recruiting for the College Section of the Council such speakers as Hans Kurath, who was to become the nation's leading dialectologist; W. A. Craigie, editor of the *Oxford English Dictionary*; Thomas A. Knott, general editor of the Merriam-Webster *Second New International Dictionary*; Edward Sapir and Leonard Bloomfield, the nation's two greatest linguists; and Sterling Andrus Leonard, who was soon to produce his influential NCTE monograph, *Current English Usage.* Their contributions were straws in the wind that in 1928 brought to the Council the significant report of its Committee on English Language Training for Teachers.

That committee's programmatic report sought, through a scientific approach, a specific means for bringing about a gradual replacement of the prevailing language mythology. The report recommended that the preparation of an English teacher include "adequate study of the historical development of English pronunciation, grammar, and vocabulary," but it continued with the revolutionary declaration that "a knowledge of the principles of general linguistics is of greater value to the teacher of English than a knowledge of the history of the language."

Unique and farseeing as the committee report turned out to be in Council history, its substance actually was not officially approved until 1951, twenty-three years later, when at the annual business meeting Fries's position was at last recognized by the following resolution:

> The National Council of Teachers of English supports the scientific study of the English language, and, realizing the importance of the results of that study in freeing our teaching from wasteful and harmful practices, recommends that, in the training of teachers, both prospective and in service, opportunities be provided to acquaint them with the principles, methods, results, and applications of modern linguistic science.... Furthermore, the National Council of Teachers of

> English believes that the schools should teach those forms of the English language which sound descriptive research has shown to be the practice of standard English in the United States.

To language scholars these statements were cogent and persuasive. But they called for a revolution in English teacher preparation, and encountered resistance in teacher-training institutions and in departments of English. To ascertain the possible effect of the 1928 statement, Fries in 1935 had obtained for me a Council research grant for a national survey of the nature of the language component in English teacher preparation. The 373 responding institutions reported a thoroughly unsatisfactory situation, one that presumably was actually worse than the responses indicated, since it is unlikely that institutions unsympathetic to the committee's statement would have responded at all. As it was, fewer than half of the 373 institutions offered coursework that could be interpreted as providing even the minimum content that the committee recommended.

But the 1951 resolution, along with some subsequent supportive articles in the Council's journals, presumably should have improved the weak response. Accordingly, to ascertain that such improvement had really occurred, in 1961 I repeated the earlier survey. During the intervening quarter of a century the situation had indeed improved in some measure, but it still had to be described as generally unsatisfactory. The results, summarized in the Council's 1961 publication *The National Interest and the Teaching of English,* revealed that, of the 569 responding institutions, fewer than 100 were graduating prospective English teachers with even minimal information about the modern study of language, and only 17 percent required a course in modern English grammar.

Clearly, certification in English was an area urgently calling for dynamic Council leadership. The efforts of Donald Tuttle, Eugene Slaughter, and Autrey Nell Wiley as successive chairs of the Committee on the Preparation and Certification of Teachers of English gave a powerful impetus to the drive for higher standards of certification in the several states, particularly with regard to the language component. Year by year that drive has continued, and some further improvement has occurred, often as a result of the influence of regional affiliates of NCTE. Yet in the absence of another survey, one suspects that inadequate preparation in language persists in many quarters, especially with respect to the preparation of teachers for the elementary schools.

The Battle of Usage

In the meantime the particular polarity between the Latinate traditional rules and the new descriptive statements about language had precipitated an oftentimes bitter conflict that some of us recall as the Battle of Usage.

Fries's 1927 book, *The Teaching of the English Language,* his step to the presidency, was followed in 1933 by Sterling Andrus Leonard's effective NCTE monograph, *Current English Usage,* and then in 1938 by another NCTE monograph, *Facts about Current English Usage,* by future NCTE president Albert H. Marckwardt and Fred G. Walcott. In the meantime the controversial but most important NCTE series, *An Experience Curriculum,* had made available to the Council an able treatment of usage by Robert C. Pooley, also a future Council president. In 1939 still another future president, Porter Perrin, broke the commercial textbook barrier with the first college freshman handbook to be based upon scientific principles of usage. Finally, in 1940, massive quantitative support came in Fries's major NCTE monograph, *American English Grammar.*

Opposition to the mounting barrage of these publications was at first overt but then consisted largely of passive resistance. By the 1950s the heavy artillery of distinguished Council leaders had won the principal vantage points, and for years an effective rearguard action was that of the monthly usage column maintained by Margaret C. Bryant in the *English Journal* and *College English.* The scientific point of view was increasingly affecting the writers of college and high school textbooks as well. Yet at the elementary level some textbooks still, in 1986, reveal the conservative stance of teachers who cling to the prescriptions of traditional grammar. Although the NCTE journal *Language Arts* has printed many articles about the language situation, unfortunately it does not reach the great mass of elementary classroom teachers. Yet ultimately it must be their voices that will affect adoption procedures and hence persuade publishers that the time has come to cease requiring children to study grammatical statements that do not fit the English language.

Officially, then, this Battle of Usage came to a close within the Council as it accepted the scientific attitude toward matters of language use. In 1963 a high point was reached when, with Priscilla Tyler as program planner, the conventions of both NCTE and the Conference on College Composition and Communication devoted major attention to a wide variety of language concerns throughout the curriculum. And in 1965 there was formed the Commission on the English Language, which has functioned as a focal point for the expression of those concerns both in programs and in publications. During the past quarter century, however, new concerns about usage, different in source and in substance, have created new polarities.

Recent Social and Theoretical Changes

The social unrest of the 1960s focused attention upon socially and educationally deprived minorities, particularly southern Black Americans whose kind of English, used in northern urban centers, became both an educational and an occupational handicap. Council journals began to respond to the new linguistic research into what was often termed Black Vernacular English, and convention programs began to provide forums for proponents and opponents of the various points of view and courses of action that had arisen. Sometimes with more heat than light, participants argued for different solutions to the educational aspects of the problem. Some demanded that the schools should stress replacement of Black English by both spoken and written standard English. Some wanted the schools to aim at developing control of spoken and written standard English but without prejudice to the continuing use of Black English when and where appropriate—a policy of bidialectalism. Others sought the development of control of edited written English without attention to spoken Black English.

Students' Right to Their Own Language

The situation rapidly became a welter of varying viewpoints with no clear polarity until action by a constituent organization within the Council, the five-thousand-member Conference on College Composition and Communication, brought matters to a head. Within its membership, consisting largely of younger instructors in college freshman English closely involved with the relevant classroom problems, a vocal and committed group led those present at a sparsely attended business meeting in 1972 to adopt by a seventy-nine-to-twenty vote a resolution designated "Students' Right to Their Own Language." The resolution, broader in scope than simply the Black English situation, was published with an explanatory policy statement in 1974. The resolution is as follows:

> We affirm the students' right to their own patterns and varieties of language—the dialects of their nurture or whatever dialects in which they find their own identity and style. Language scholars long ago denied that the myth of a standard American dialect has any validity. The claim that any one dialect is unacceptable amounts to an attempt of one social group to exert its dominance over another. Such a claim leads to false advice for speakers and writers, and immoral advice for humans. A nation proud of its diverse heritage and its cultural and racial variety will preserve its heritage of dialects. We affirm that teachers must have the experiences and training that will enable them to respect diversity and uphold the right of students to their own language.

In the same year the Council itself, in a less-than-unanimous vote, adopted a form of the resolution modified so as to distinguish between spoken and written English and to support providing opportunities for learning to control the conventions of edited written English.

Official support of the resolution did not, however, resolve the polarity. Speakers and writers within the Council criticized the ambiguity of the unexplained term *right* and raised questions about the difficulties likely to be encountered in classroom implementation. No attempts were made to rescind the resolution, but in 1981 NCTE president William Irmscher wrote to CCCC chair Lynn Quitman Troyka to suggest that, without prejudice to the *Students' Right* document, a new CCCC committee be formed to evaluate priorities concerning the use of language forms different from those in dominant standard English. The resulting committee, named in 1982, was charged "to decide whether recent findings and developments in multilingualism and multidialectalism make it desirable for CCCC to prepare a statement on language for the 1980s and 1990s." The committee eventually reached consensus (except for one dissident) in a report to the CCCC executive committee in 1983. The report approved retention of the original *Students' Right* resolution but pointed out that, since the committee was an agent of an organization constitutionally limited to concern with problems of college composition, it felt unable to deal with the complex problem as a whole. It pointed out that the problem must be approached in teacher training and in the elementary schools, and therefore requested the CCCC executive committee to ask the Council itself to set up a task force with adequate input from linguists, sociologists, and psychologists as well as from other areas of the English profession, the task force to study thoroughly the most effective means of implementing the resolution with respect both to the profession and to the concerned public. At a special meeting of the CCCC executive committee in November 1983, the report of the special committee was tabled and hence was never submitted to the CCCC membership. There is no quantitative evidence as to the effect the *Students' Right* statement has had upon teacher training or upon teaching in the elementary and secondary schools.

The TESOL Controversy

A related controversy arose after the creation of Teachers of English to Speakers of Other Languages (TESOL) in 1966. TESOL would presumably free NCTE from concern for students with a first language other than English. But with the development of bilingual education programs, partly because of federal action, English teachers often found themselves facing students who had emerged from bilingual programs without enough control of English to move into mainstream English classes. Questions arose as to the role of NCTE with respect to the various options offered in many schools: sustained maintenance of the first language, use of the first language only until students move into regular English classes, or tutorial assistance outside of usual class hours. Another option was to ignore the problem by letting the students get along as best they could, especially when a given class contained only two or three low-English-proficiency students who might even come from widely varying language backgrounds. NCTE two years later adopted a position paper supporting a program leading eventually to sole use of English in school but also to providing at least minimal help to teachers lacking any professional training in teaching English as a second language.

Sexist Language

A third recent issue engendered in the social turmoil of the 1960s concerned what has become known as sexist language. A swiftly growing wave of protest developed against the centuries-old lexical differentiation between the sexes when it served only to preserve the values of a male-dominated social order. Just as in churches the protest called for the adoption of "inclusive language," so in NCTE it demanded the removal in general discourse of all vocabulary and grammatical features using the male term to mean people of both sexes or needlessly distinguishing male from female, and unmarried from married women. So *Miss* and *Mrs.* were to be replaced by *Ms., chairman* and *chairwoman* by *chair* or *chairperson, policeman* by *police officer,* and the "generic" *he* and *him* by *he or she, him or her, they,* or *them* if at all possible. The Council accepted such changes without major internal controversy except for a successful plea from anti-censorship proponents that authors of books and contributors to journals who wished to retain the older forms should be allowed to do so, with a printed disclaimer that the language was to stand at the express stipulation of the author. But the larger issues of sexism in language remain a fertile field for further investigation and research with regard to far-reaching personal and social and political implications, and the Council has published articles and pamphlets examining some of these implications.

Doublespeak

In line with this same interest in the social and political implications of language, perhaps the Council activity which has achieved greatest publicity is the annual award of the NCTE Committee on Public Doublespeak. Formed to throw light upon the unethical use of the language by public figures or organizations, the committee utilizes the NCTE convention as the occasion to publicize its choices of the most flagrant violators of language ethics during the preceding year. Twice the committee has demonstrated its freedom from external control by finding that the most flagrant user of dishonesty in language was President Ronald Reagan.

Transformational/Generative Grammar

A quite different source of NCTE language concerns lay in the set of linguistic theories known as transformational or generative grammar, developed from the original brief presentation by the linguist Noam Chomsky in his book *Linguistic Structures* in 1957. Although transformational grammar drew professional attention in Council journals, it has not replaced in school textbooks either the reformed versions of traditional grammar or the various syntactic treatments derived from structural grammar as analyzed in Fries's *The Structure of English* in 1952 or the W. Nelson Francis textbook for prospective English teachers, *The Structure of American English,* published in 1958. But transformational grammar has been influential because of its emphasis upon the underlying patterns of the language from which surface structures may be derived. It thus has led to research in sentence combining as a means of helping students to attain control of a mature style, to a new analysis of rhetorical theory, and to new insights in literary criticism. A number of Council publications and convention papers reflect those concerns.

In this overview of the Council and the English language, much has been slighted and even omitted, especially the proliferation of language interests during the past twenty-five years. But it should be clear from even this brief report that, for the profession of English teaching, the National Council of Teachers of English has become the leading power to draw upon linguistic scholarship for what is valuable in English education. Through all its activity, NCTE has amply demonstrated that the English language is indeed the bedrock of the profession.

Reference

Greenbaum, Sidney, ed., *The English Language Today* (Oxford: Pergamon Institute, 1985).

2 Reading/Literature

Rudine Sims

That this chapter should be titled "Reading/Literature" and not "Reading Literature" is itself an indication of one of the most important dichotomies within the profession. It signifies our preoccupation at the elementary level with the *how* of reading, and our tendency at higher levels to define literature as a body of knowledge to be acquired, rather than a means of exploring and expanding our insights into what it means to be human. On the one hand we are beset with articles and books on "using literature to teach reading," while on the other the lament is, "How can we teach literature if they don't know how to read?"

This dichotomy between the what and the how, between the means and the ends, has not always been so pronounced. When the Old Deluder Satan Act required the establishment of schools in seventeenth-century Massachusetts, the colonists were certain of the purpose they wished literacy to serve: to see that the children were able to read the Bible and other religious material, to ensure that their souls would be saved. Content was all-important. This preoccupation with the content of reading texts continued through the period following the American Revolution, when the focus was on "nationalizing" the citizens of the new nation; and through most of the nineteenth century, when the concern was ensuring an intelligent electorate. By the end of the nineteenth century, reading was being viewed as a cultural asset, as a means to cultivate good taste in literature, and there were complaints about the lack of real literature in the reading texts of the day. Thus the focus on teaching literature as a separate subject has a relatively brief history in the United States.

From about the middle of the nineteenth century on, influenced by information from abroad and spurred by our own burgeoning educational research efforts, increasing attention was given to the importance of methodology in teaching reading. By the middle of the twentieth century, following a period of intense scientific investigation and the Sputnik crisis, the great debate in reading was couched only in terms of methodology: whether "look-say" or "decoding" was the better way to teach beginning reading.

While newer knowledge is tending to reunite the study of reading and literature, the fact is that the two remain separate in our curriculum planning and our thinking. Significantly, NCTE maintains both a Commission on Reading and a Commission on Literature. The disciplines of the literature teacher and the reading teacher may overlap, but their dissimilar preservice education and their differing job descriptions lead to different expectations and different concerns. Therefore, this essay will examine each of the areas separately.

Reading: Major Developments and Influences

A Knowledge Explosion

The past quarter of a century has seen a virtual explosion of knowledge and information about reading and the reading process. Linguists provided information and theories about how language works and about how young children learn it, and the linguists' view of language learners as active makers of meaning and constructors of grammars influenced those reading theorists who saw reading as a parallel language process. Some cognitive psychologists, psycholinguists, and educational theorists created models of the reading process itself, suggesting implications for the learning and teaching of reading. Others began to study and analyze texts and how they are put together and understood, developing such techniques as story grammars and propositional analyses. More recently, educators have rediscovered the field of semiotics, and are finding information there which sheds light on the study of language in use.

Some of the new information has come from within the field of reading itself. Influenced by information from psychologists and psycholinguists, some educational researchers began to study reading by examining the miscues made during oral reading. These studies led to new insights about the reading process, and eventually to newer suggestions for assessing reading proficiency. Other researchers, influenced by the studies of oral language development, began to look at early literacy development, and to discover that, just as children learn much about oral language before schooling, children in a print-filled society also learn much about written language prior to school entry.

All of this information about language and language processing has created a new context for the debates about curriculum and methodology. Most of the information does not translate directly into curriculum or methodology, but it often becomes the theoretical foundation for new research, and, eventually, new curricular schemes. At minimum, it has helped us to comprehend the great complexity involved in understanding written language, and led us to a greater respect for readers as language learners and language users.

Qualitative Research/The Teacher as Researcher

As researchers in reading have learned more about language and language learning and have become convinced of the social nature of language as well as the importance of context in its development and use, they have begun to turn to naturalistic research techniques, most notably ethnographic techniques, borrowed from anthropology. The participant observer has arrived in the classroom. One result of the increased presence of researchers in the classroom has been a recognition that the teacher is far more valuable as a co-researcher than as a mere subject of research. This trend has great promise, not only as a means of gathering more information about how language is learned and used in the classroom but also as a means of keeping informed teachers at the center of curricular decision making.

Reading and the Home

The trend toward naturalistic research has also led to a consideration of language learning in contexts other than classrooms, most notably the home. Recent research has concentrated on the preschool years, and has helped us to confirm the crucial role that parents play in their children's written language development. Researchers have discovered, too, that even those children who do not grow up in advantaged, book-filled homes have many experiences daily with print, and that from those experiences they learn something about written language in general and, in particular, about how it functions in their social group. Parents are thus their children's first teachers, partners in literacy development.

Curriculum and Teaching

It would be unusual indeed if some of the knowledge generated over the past quarter century about language and language learning had not begun to have some influence on the classroom and the curriculum in reading. Interestingly, the fundamental debate about methodology still continues, couched today in terms of "whole language" vs. "skills" approaches. Tradition, teachers' manuals, and certain theoretical models of the reading process suggest that reading is a composite of a number of skills, and that learning to read is a matter of acquiring those skills in some logical sequence. Consequently, instructional materials and programs are created to develop those skills, and teachers are expected to see that students master them. Not until students have passed through a "learning to read" stage and into a "reading to learn" stage does content become as important as methodology. On the other side of the debate are those who see reading, like all language processes, as a process of making meaning. They insist that instructional materials from the very beginning must present real language, and that as the learner learns to take care of the sense, the skills will take care of themselves. Rather than teaching skills, these theorists want to help readers develop strategies for making sense of written language. Therefore, part of the promise of the "whole language" position is that the content of reading materials becomes important once again, and literature becomes central to any good reading program.

Today's teacher of reading must also be concerned with other aspects of the language curriculum. One "in" aspect of language today is writing, the result of another part of the knowledge explosion. Not only have we rediscovered writing, but we have also begun to examine the reading/writing connection. Moreover, since we understand that every encounter with language, whether in a receptive or productive mode, adds to our store of knowledge about how language works, *oral* language also becomes an important aspect of the curriculum. The trend today is to turn our English classrooms into literate environments where students and teachers read and write and talk and listen daily, and where students and teachers in workshop-like settings respond to each other's work.

Another current trend is toward what is called "language across the curriculum." We recognize that, except perhaps when we make a study of language itself, language is always *for* something, and cannot be taught effectively in isolation. Each discipline in the school curriculum has its own characteristic ways of using language, as well as its own vocabulary. While the attempt to have every teacher see him- or herself as a teacher of reading has never been entirely successful, we continue to recognize that content-area teachers play an important role in helping students learn to understand and use language appropriately in all disciplines. Language use is not confined to the English classroom, and we will need to continue to enlist the aid of colleagues in other disciplines.

Finally, teachers of reading today are faced with accusations that we have done our job so poorly that the nation is faced once again with a literacy crisis. There is a cry for adult literacy programs to aid the estimated millions of so-called functional illiterates. Closer to the classroom, there is a cry for standardized testing programs to assure the American public that we are doing our jobs properly. Over the past several years, however, we have learned much about the complexities of language, and about the inability of current standardized tests to reflect a student's understanding of that complexity. There is a danger that the pressures to prepare students to pass minimal competency tests will have an adverse effect on the teaching of reading, encouraging attention to quantifiable and simplistic skills and discouraging teachers from providing the kinds of experiences with language and literature that, according to our best current knowledge, are most valuable for language learners.

Literature: Issues, Influences, and Developments

Recent Influences and Developments

The teaching of literature in the United States continues to be influenced by the British curriculum models observed and discussed in the sixties. The Anglo-American Seminar on the Teaching of English, held at Dartmouth in 1966, brought together about fifty American and British experts in English education to discuss common issues in the field. The British concern with process as opposed to content, and with student growth, rather than with the "covering" of certain texts; their extensive use of drama in the classroom; and their use of modern literature as opposed to a prescribed set of literary texts have all found their way into the professional literature, if not into all of the English classrooms of this country.

Another relatively recent trend in the teaching of literature, one related to the British model as well as to the earlier progressive movement in U.S. education, is the emphasis on response to literature, which is the subject of much of the current research in the field. This emphasis on response is also related to current views on the nature of the reading experience itself, greatly influenced by Louise Rosenblatt's 1938 book *Literature as Exploration* (3d ed., New York: Noble and Noble, 1976), and her more recent *The Reader, the Text, the Poem* (Carbondale: Southern Illinois Univ. Press, 1978; both distributed by NCTE). What Rosenblatt and those who share her views stress is that the reader, together with the text, creates the literary work—neither does it alone. This emphasis on the significant role of the reader lends itself to studying the responses of children in the lower elementary grades, heretofore largely neglected since so much past research relied on paper-and-pencil measures.

Another current research interest in the field of literature is the study of narratology. Just as researchers in reading have discovered semiotics, they also have discovered narratology, the structural analysis of narrative or story. Renewed interest in this field promises to restore story/literature, the content of reading, to a central place in the elementary language arts curriculum. Interestingly, at the same time that researchers are studying the structure of stories, storytelling itself seems to be making a comeback in the field of English language arts. Increasing numbers of workshops and convention sessions indicate a resurgence of interest in this traditional art, which encourages students and teachers both to enjoy this oral tradition for its own sake and to use it as a foundation on which to build greater interest in and understanding of written literature.

What Should Students Read?

The emphasis on response to literature is countered by other concerns, among them the question of what works students should be reading in the English classroom. Recent school reformers suggest that part of the reason for the perceived widespread near-illiteracy of our students is the proliferation of English electives. There is a sense that students have not been subjected to the intellectual discipline it takes to understand serious literature, and instead have been permitted to spend their time reading easily accessible modern fluff. Therefore, say the critics, they do not know how to read literature, they have little interest in doing so, and they are almost totally unfamiliar with their own literary heritage. These critics' remedies point toward a return to the required reading of certain "classics," a kind of core of cultural experience that all high school graduates should have. Judging from the 1985 edition of NCTE's Classroom Practices in the Teaching of English (*Literature—News That Stays News: Fresh Approaches to the Classics*), English teachers regularly present such literature; the classics have never been abandoned.

At the same time, many English teachers recognize that a literature curriculum that concentrates entirely on so-called classics has the disadvantage of excluding the rich multicultural literature that is part of the heritage of many of the students in our schools. Most frequently, the preferred "classical" experience is the standard literature and history of the Western world, meaning that, unfortunately, lists of suggested classics tend to exclude literature by and about people of color and women, and, by definition, anything that has not stood the test of time. In many cases the maligned electives are an attempt to allow students to experience the common themes and ideas found in good literature in the context of literary works that recreate characters, settings, and problems that today's students can find familiar.

One source of such experience is the current abundance of literature for children and adolescents. While some critics rightly point out the flaws in many so-called problem novels for adolescents, and decry the tendency in many such novels for the problems to outweigh the literary quality, others recognize the high literary quality of works by such authors as Robert Cormier, Katherine Paterson, Virginia Hamilton, Paul Zindel, Isaac Asimov, and many others. There is today a plethora of high-quality literature written for children and adolescents. Its availability in paperback editions permits many teachers to use adolescent literature, along with some of the classics, in thematic units during which students confront and discuss some of the eternal and perhaps universal themes that recur in good literature.

However, not all of the literature currently being published for young people is of such high quality. Mindful of competition from television and other media, publishers have produced a flood of drugstore romances for teen and preteen readers, as well as a number of game books in which the real point may not be the experience of reading itself, but the playing or winning of the game. The other unhappy news about much available contemporary literature is that the quantity of ethnic literature, particularly about people of color in the United States, has greatly diminished since the heyday of the seventies. Fortunately, however, the *quality* of such literature has risen over the past twenty years and remains high. The decrease in the quantity of ethnic literature may be partly a reflection of the conservative social climate of the eighties, a climate which has also enlivened the debate over censorship.

Censorship vs. Selection

Soon after the 1980 presidential elections, the American Library Association noted a substantial increase in the number of censorship cases brought to its attention. Teaching literature is on some level always a political act, since we believe in the power of the word to influence the minds and hearts of our students. Therefore, a politically conservative segment of the population perceives the English classroom as a place where their values may be threatened and countered with antithetical ones. This has led to many attempts to ban books—from dictionaries to *Walden*. On the other side of the political fence, there are pressures on English teachers to include the literature of so-called minorities and to exclude literature which perpetuates racism, sexism, and other -isms abhorrent to people who like to call themselves humanists. Typically, it is most often English teachers who find themselves embroiled in controversy.

One way many English teachers use to get around such controversies is to grant students some choice in the literature they will read. The provision of alternative selections often reduces attempts at censorship because no student is required to read a work that either the student or his or her parents find offensive. Many schools have developed policies and procedures for dealing with potentially controversial selections, and have found these instruments helpful to teachers in the avoidance of censorship challenges. Possibly the most dangerous consequences of censorship controversies is that we will begin to practice self-censorship, and so end up with a bland, quite safe, but totally irrelevant literature curriculum.

Conclusion

Our profession continues to regard literature and reading as separate aspects of the English curriculum. Reading instruction occupies a large proportion of the elementary school day, particularly in the primary grades. While professional leaders urge teachers to use more literature in the context of reading programs, basal readers continue to be the major determinant of both how reading is taught and what material is read, and skill instruction predominates. At the secondary level, reading programs are still largely perceived as skills programs for those who did not gain enough reading proficiency in elementary school. One of the problems we need to solve is how to make the reading of literature one of the central aspects of the elementary language arts curriculum, and how to expand the notion of developing reading proficiency into one that does not stop at the end of sixth grade.

Current research and developments suggest that in language arts classrooms of the future there will be much emphasis on the social nature of language and language learning, including the learning of written language. The focus will be on creating literate environments in which students and teachers read, write, and talk to each other daily about issues of concern to them and to the society at large. On the other hand, the impact of modern technology is not yet clear. Advances in film, television, and computers may indeed change some of the ways we use written language, but it is doubtful that written literacy will disappear in the near future.

Today's teacher of reading and literature works in an atmosphere of mixed messages: abundant high-quality literature for children and adolescents continues to be published, but monies for libraries are being drastically cut; much exciting research is being carried out, and its results disseminated, but school districts and conservative community leaders continue to cling to traditional methods and materials; reformers demand excellence in teaching, but want to hold teachers accountable by using tests which cannot adequately assess the desired results of excellent programs. Thus today more than ever the burden of professional decision making falls heavily on the shoulders of individual teachers, who, buffeted by a sea of contradictory information, must nevertheless daily find ways to help young people experience the joy and wonder to be found in reading literature.

3 Written Composition: Progress and the Search for Paradigms

Paul T. Bryant

As we celebrate the seventy-fifth anniversary of the National Council of Teachers of English, we are in the best of times and the worst of times for teachers of written composition. It is the best of times for new ideas, new knowledge, new ways of teaching; it is the worst of times for stability, coherence, generally shared assumptions about the writing process, in short, for a broadly accepted paradigm.

As teachers of English, we are in a situation now somewhat like that of biological scientists in the nineteenth century. Then, biologists did not know molecular chemistry and subatomic physics; they lacked scanning electron microscopes, cell sorters, and computers. As a result, their study of living organisms was limited to relatively rudimentary techniques of observation, description, and classification.

Composition is at much the same stage now. Our knowledge in psychology, linguistics, and communication theory is still too limited to support the development and testing of complex theories concerning the process of composition, so we must rely on relatively simple observation, description, and classification. We should not push the analogy too far, but the similarities may be instructive as we struggle to lay a strong foundation. Biologists have their Darwin, Wallace, and Huxley, and we are developing our major figures, too.

From Rhetoric to Etiquette and Back

This current surge of interest in, and study of, composition has been with us for only twenty years or so. In the history of education in this country, writing has moved from the very center, to a peripheral code of etiquette, and, perhaps, now back to the center again. Classical rhetoric has a long tradition in Western civilization, but early rhetorical instruction at Harvard, our first college, was not classical. Rather, it was based on the ideas of Peter Ramee and Omer Talon, reformers who had broken up the five elements of the classical rhetorical tradition—invention, arrangement, style, memory, and delivery—by putting invention and arrangement under logic.[1] Thus the first "revival" of classical rhetoric in America did not come until the eighteenth century. As might be expected, in that time of democratic political turmoil rhetoric's importance lay in public discourse. By the nineteenth century, however, at least partly because of a new emphasis on literature, rhetoric began a decline.[2] This decline continued in American education at least through the first two decades of this century. "Speech" became a separate field, providing the most active teachers of classical rhetoric. Composition, more and more separated from the rhetorical tradition, focused primarily on style.[3]

By the 1940s, the teaching of composition clearly needed new life, new ideas, and these began to appear. There was the communications movement that attempted to reunite the basic skills of speaking, writing, listening, and reading. And there was the semantics movement. Both had promise, but neither finally was fully adequate to the need.[4] In the 1950s and 1960s interest grew in structural linguistics, generative and transformational grammar, and behavior modification through programmed learning. But still, in 1963, Albert Kitzhaber could write, "Freshman English in the nation's colleges and universities is now so confused, so clearly in need of radical and sweeping reforms, that college English departments can continue to ignore the situation only at their increasing peril."[5] Although linguists had by then begun to produce much new knowledge about language, Kitzhaber found that most current handbooks were still largely prescriptive and that few tried to present even a small part of this knowledge.[6]

At this low point for the teaching of composition, the seeds of coming change had already been sown. As early as 1931 Kenneth Burke had begun the development of a rhetorical approach to writing with *Counter-Statement.* The neo-Aristotelians at Chicago became active. In 1950 Burke's *A Rhetoric of Motives* appeared, and in 1959 Daniel Fogarty's *Roots of a New Rhetoric.* In the 1960s there were Edward P. J. Corbett's *Classical Rhetoric for the Modern Student* (1965) and Martin Steinmann's *New Rhetoric* (1967).

Also during the sixties the Dartmouth Conference advocated developmental goals for the English curriculum, focusing on increased self-awareness, an approach criticized by some for its emphasis on emotional self-expression without adequate attention to writing as a social or transactional activity.[7] Nevertheless, the conference did stimulate discussion of the major questions Kitzhaber and others said must be addressed if teaching composition were to be revitalized, and it helped to make the 1960s a pivotal decade.

Beginning the Renaissance

Since then we have seen a major revival of interest in rhetoric, growing to some extent out of a sense of the sterility of the prescriptive "handbook etiquette" of the thirties and forties. With this renewal of interest in rhetoric we have again turned attention to invention, arrangement, style, and the relationship of writer to reader as well as topic. We have shifted our pedagogical emphasis from analyzing (correcting) the product to understanding and assisting in the process of writing. We have in effect turned from criticism to teaching.

A major figure in this renewed attention to rhetoric, as already suggested, has been Kenneth Burke, with his dramatistic analysis of the writing process into the pentad of act, scene, agent, agency, and purpose. In his emphasis on the relational nature of communication, Burke "looms as a gray eminence over all contemporary studies in discourse, communication theory, and semiotics."[8]

Although Burke has perhaps had greater influence in speech communication than in composition, James Moffett has provided a relational discourse theory that deals directly with written discourse. Burke did not substantially demonstrate the value of his pentad in analysis of specific written discourse, but Moffett's theory has clear pedagogical applications both in examining the writer's relationship with the audience and with the topic.[9] Moffett's applications draw on the research of Jean Piaget, using the Piagetian spectrum of writer-reader relationship from egocentric to decentered.

Not all of the new rhetorical approaches are relational. Those by Frank D'Angelo and James Kinneavy, for example, are categorical systems that can help teachers define the often incomplete writing intentions of their students.[10] Kinneavy's *A Theory of Discourse* (1971) is essentially Aristotelian in its approach, bringing classical rhetorical principles into modern rhetorical thought.[11]

Even as teachers of composition began to move away from the teaching of grammar and an emphasis on "correctness," linguists began to develop new concepts of how language works. In each case, however, the usefulness of their ideas was limited in the actual teaching of writing. Structural grammar focused on linguistic performance and did not consider the mental processes involved. Structuralists began with sounds and worked up to the sentence, a limited range for the teacher of writing. Generative/transformational grammarians began with the sentence and tried to explain how speakers can construct infinitely variable sentences.[12] Out of this approach grew sentence combining, a significant development in the rhetoric of the sentence that was foreshadowed by Francis Christensen's generative rhetoric of the sentence. Although Christensen's approach contains linguistic ambiguities, it has practical value for teaching composition. For students at a certain level in the development of their writing, sentence combining has provided teachers with a major pedagogical tool.[13] Still, while studies at the sentence level and below may help students develop more flexibility in sentence structure, and should make them better editors, it may not help them learn to write.[14] We have begun to realize that writing involves far more than the manipulation or construction of discrete linguistic structures.

From Product to Process

By the 1970s, then, the field of composition was in a ferment. New insights and new ideas were coming from many directions: from psychology, linguistics, rhetoric, speech, logic and information theory, philosophy. As emphasis shifted from the analysis of the *product* of writing—the study of the static artifact—to the analysis and ultimately the direction of the *process* of writing, an enterprise that was dynamic, almost protean, dozens of new avenues of investigation opened. At the same time, the enormous complexity of the subject became more and more apparent. Coherence and a community of scholarly effort among widely disparate groups became essential to keep the ferment from degenerating into a babel. A keynote address at the 1973 annual meeting of the Conference on College Composition and Communication called for composition teachers and researchers to become more aware of, and build more directly upon, the body of knowledge that had already been developed in the field.[15] Gary Tate responded to that call with his landmark volume, *Teaching Composition: Ten Bibliographic Essays* (1976). Since that publication, there have been a number of significant bibliographic projects by Winifred Horner, Richard Larson, and others, which have begun to provide teachers and researchers in composition the necessary bibliographic tools to trace developments in the field and to build in a systematic way on the work already done. Although bibliographic resources comparable to those available to literary scholars are not yet at hand, interest in developing such tools is high. A number of significant bibliographic projects are now in progress and should soon contribute to the development and coherent organization of knowledge in the field.

With the shift of attention from product to process in writing, analysis of writing has taken several forms. Stages in the process have been variously identified, but basically they are prewriting, writing, and revising.

Other schemes consider preparation (conceptualizing), incubation (development), and production (both writing and revising).[16] By breaking this complex process into steps, we can more easily study each. The danger, of course, is that we will begin to regard the entire process as linear, although evidence is overwhelming that the writing process is recursive. Thus any designation of stages, convenient though it may be, is arbitrary and distorts the true nature of what a writer does. Nevertheless, structuring is a step that is probably necessary for teaching the process, one aspect at a time, rather than resorting to the old, nonteaching approach of having the student write (i.e., perform all stages of the process for each assignment) and then only evaluating the result.

Of these various stages, one that has received much attention is invention. Although it is one of the categories in classical rhetoric (the topoi), approaches to invention in recent years have drawn heavily on psychological research. This research has led us to view writing as a way to explore, understand, and finally provide a structure for experience. The act of composition thus becomes a process of discovery; invention becomes more than a way to rework known materials. Various invention heuristics have begun to find a place in composition texts.

Some heuristics function in narrowly problem-oriented ways, such as the traditional journalist's standard series: who, what, when, where, how? When the writing task is limited and straightforward in purpose—reporting an event for the news media, reporting the results of a scientific experiment—such problem-oriented heuristics work well, but they clearly limit the "discovery" aspect of invention. Other heuristics, however, such as Kenneth Burke's "dramatistic" pentad (act, scene, agent, agency, purpose), Gregory and Elizabeth Cowan's looping and cubing exercises, and Richard Larson's problem-solving model, provide more flexible techniques for writers attempting to discover what they have to say.[17]

Another approach to the process is through the particular skills required of the student at each stage. These have been classified as "open" and "closed" skills.[18] Closed skills include the mechanical operations of editing for correctness in spelling, punctuation, and grammar. These can be fully completed tasks; a piece of writing can be without mechanical error. Open capacities, on the other hand, are such activities as invention, development, organization, and revision. These operations can be done better or worse, but there is no absolute closure, nor is there a single, absolute standard against which they can be evaluated. The effective writing instructor must understand which elements of the process require open capacities and which closed, and develop methods for teaching each.

Piaget, Emig, and Britton

Jean Piaget, perhaps the most significant researcher in developmental psychology, has also influenced the teaching of writing. His study of the stages of learning through which a child passes from birth to late adolescence—the cognitive stages of childhood—has provided a scale by which to match writing assignments to the development of students. From the sensory-motor stage of the infant, through preoperational thought (ability to symbolize experience), concrete operations (growing capacity for abstraction), and the final stage of formal operations, language provides an indicator of a student's development and helps the child progress. Language for Piaget has two functions: it can help the child develop increasingly complex cognitions; then, through "decentering," it helps the child understand other visions of reality. Through language the child can escape from "cognitive egocentrism."[19]

Two particular studies in recent years have become reference points for our knowledge of the composing process: James Britton et al., *The Development of Writing Abilities (11–18),* and Janet Emig, *The Composing Processes of Twelfth Graders.*[20] In his approach to a useful paradigm for composition, Britton has postulated three categories of discourse, on the basis of function. If the writing is intended to cause something to happen (inform, persuade, influence the reader in some way), it is transactional writing. If the writing examines experience to understand it or determine its value, the writing becomes an end in itself and is considered poetic. These are the two ends of the spectrum. Between these ends is the most personal and immediate writing, which assumes a close relationship between writer and audience (they may indeed be the same). This Britton calls expressive writing.

School children, Britton says, should begin with expressive writing. From there, as the student moves through the stages of development, writing assignments can progress in level of complexity and abstractness, and to addressing less-personally-known audiences. In addressing progressively less-known audiences, the student "decenters" attention from self to others.

Janet Emig identifies patterns much like Britton's, but she calls them reflexive and extensive. She also offers alternative views of creativity in writing, and calls attention to the affective and cognitive dimensions of writing.

A New Clientele

As these new approaches were beginning to form in the early seventies, and as the old certainties of handbook etiquette and Latinate grammar were discounted or destroyed, many teachers were struggling for the first time with a flood of students who in the past might never have reached the higher levels of our educational system. Integration, the burgeoning of community colleges, and open admissions at many institutions were presenting composition teachers with students from a much wider range, both culturally and linguistically, than before. Dialects seldom heard before in high school or college became commonplace, and changing cultural and linguistic attitudes were helping to establish their validity. Nevertheless, the writing teacher was expected to teach these students to write standard academic prose.

There was little in the history of composition that could directly help these teachers with this monumental, and monumentally significant, new task. Then Mina Shaughnessy published *Errors and Expectations* in 1977, and a new approach was offered that was in harmony with current linguistic knowledge. What she offered was error analysis. Rather than assuming in basic writing that errors are to be identified (pointed out to the students) and corrected, Shaughnessy postulated that the *cause* of the error is more important then the *fact* of the error. The teacher should assume that there is some reasonable cause for the error in the student's background and knowledge of the language. If the teacher can discover why the student has made the error, then the teacher can help the student understand and control the habits or perceptions that caused the error, thus possibly making the "error" a positive element in the development of the student's writing. Error analysis has provided a significant and fruitful area of investigation in our agenda.

Across the Curriculum

Another important development in moving writing from the academic periphery back to the heart of intellectual growth has been renewed emphasis on "writing across the curriculum." Teachers in most fields will agree that a student should know how to write well, but most are willing to leave that teaching responsibility to the English department. Essays take longer to read and are harder to grade than problems or multiple-choice or true/false tests. It is hard enough teaching history or chemistry or mathematics without having to help do the English teacher's job, too. Or such has been a common view. But now educational psychologists and composition researchers are turning that argument the other way. Teachers of all subjects, they say, should be requiring their students to write, not to help English teachers, *but to help themselves.* Writing has been shown to be a powerful tool in the learning process.

Emig has asserted that the effectiveness of writing as a learning tool lies in the extent to which the learning process and the writing process are parallel. Both are multifaceted, recursive, using eye, mind, and hand, right- and left-brain functions. Both are analytical and synthesizing.[21] Various studies have demonstrated both this enhancement of learning and the value of writing in helping students progress through Piaget's levels of intellectual development.[22] Jerome Bruner, another advocate of cognitive psychology who has drawn heavily on the work of Piaget, regards language as an instrument of thought, and syntax as a mode of organizing experience. Armed with this concept and the supporting data, writing teachers can now go to teachers of other subjects with a very meaningful offer to help *them* with *their* teaching responsibilities.

Reunion with Literary Study

Yet another development that gives promise of restoring writing to its old place at the center of education is the developing trend to restore nonfiction prose to a significant place in the literary canon. As Richard Lloyd-Jones, president of NCTE in this, our Diamond Jubilee year, has observed, "When we defined nonfiction out of literature and tried to restrict ourselves to teaching poetry and fiction, we distorted the nature of discourse as it exists and as it is important to a healthy society. The study of English should encompass all kinds of uses; our value to the academy and the society is that we study the mechanism which controls the perceptions of individual people and allows them to pool their experience into a common understanding. Writing and reading in the full sense define humanity."[23] This is the point at which rhetoric and literary criticism may again connect, reuniting those sometimes schizophrenic sides of so many English departments.

These are indeed, then, stimulating, challenging, and hopeful times for writing teachers. Gone is the sense that our teaching is the hopeless drudgery of correcting spelling, punctuation, and grammar, knowing full well we will see the same errors, made by the same students, next week. By changing our focus to the process of writing, we have opened the door to productive investigation. When we looked only at the product of writing, we could give our students primarily affective judgments and engage in analysis only after the fact, and in the end we had only more information about work already written. We had no more information about *how* it was written. So our studies could only supply us with more complex models for our students. We could not tell them how to go about emulating the models. Now, as we gain knowledge about how writing occurs, we can offer our students more help in the process of writing.

The millenium in composition has not yet arrived, however. We still face challenges, problems, pitfalls. We still have much to learn and will undoubtedly encounter frustrations, mistakes, dead ends, and disagreements. We still are divided in many ways. For example, as we shift our attention to process, we are more and more teaching writing as a "studio" or "laboratory" course concerned with doing something rather than talking about it. Yet we still schedule and often conduct our classes as if they were "lectures," giving us neither the setting nor the time needed to do the kind of teaching we want to do.

Again, we are not yet clear on what we mean by "good" writing. What are we trying to teach our students to do? Do we want them to learn the conventions of writing? Creative self-expression? Clarity? Elegance? Effective communication? If communication, what should they be able to communicate: data, opinion, belief, concepts, emotional experience, or all of the above?

Types of Theories

As we develop or consider various theories of discourse, we must also learn to make distinctions among the natures of those theories. They are not all theories in the scientific sense of hypotheses that can be tested objectively. Many offer only a more or less arbitrary structuring of descriptive analysis; many are creative metaphors designed to offer conceptual arrangement of complex phenomena. We must learn to distinguish among these various types, because a testable statement of objective physical fact requires a different response from an artistic conceptual metaphor.

Even those theories that can be objectively tested are not always then so tested, as indicated by the example of Robert Zoellner's behavioral approach to teaching composition, a complex but eminently testable hypothesis. For a time after its publication in *College English* in 1969 it was surrounded by a storm of debate, but more than fifteen years later there does not appear to have been any objective testing of that hypothesis, either by Zoellner or by those who opposed his ideas.

Another hazard of the scientific approach for teachers of writing who were not originally educated as scientists is that we will use outdated science. Just as some literary critics have used the theories of Freud and Jung as the last word in the psychological interpretation of literature, long after psychologists have gone far beyond Freud and Jung, so we may be tempted to use the work of Vygotsky or Piaget as the "gospel" in psychology long after cognitive psychologists have gone far beyond that work. To avoid such an error, we must remember to include psychologists in our research.

As we approach the study of writing, and the teaching of writing, we must understand when our approach is aesthetic, when psychoanalytical, when descriptive, when metaphoric. If we do not keep such distinctions in mind, we may find it difficult to communicate even among ourselves.

Toward a New Paradigm

In the February 1982 issue of *College Composition and Communication* Maxine Hairston's article, "The Winds of Change: Thomas Kuhn and the Revolution in the Teaching of Writing," discussed the new paradigm that is developing for composition. Using the definition of a theoretical paradigm presented in Kuhn's *The Structure of Scientific Revolutions,* that it is a common body of beliefs and assumptions held by most practitioners in a field, Hairston concluded that the teaching of composition is in the midst of a paradigm shift, a period in which the old paradigm is no longer adequate and people in the field are searching for a new one that accommodates our present knowledge. She presents twelve features of the emerging paradigm:

1. It focuses on the writing process; instructors intervene in students' writing during the process.
2. It teaches strategies for invention and discovery; instructors help students to generate content and discover purpose.
3. It is rhetorically based; audience, purpose, and occasion figure prominently in the assignment of writing tasks.
4. Instructors evaluate the written product by how well it fulfills the writer's intention and meets the audience's needs.
5. It views writing as a recursive rather than a linear process; prewriting, writing, and revision are activities that overlap and intertwine.
6. It is holistic, viewing writing as an activity that involves the intuitive and non-rational as well as the rational faculties.
7. It emphasizes that writing is a way of learning and developing as well as a communication skill.
8. It includes a variety of writing modes, expressive as well as expository.
9. It is informed by other disciplines, especially cognitive psychology and linguistics.
10. It views writing as a disciplined creative activity that can be analyzed and described; its practitioners believe that writing can be taught.
11. It is based on linguistic research and research into the composing process.
12. It stresses the principle that writing teachers should be people who write.[24]

Others in the field might add or take away items from this list, but something is emerging that is very like these points in aggregate.

Out of the ferment, the debate, the dissatisfaction with the old and the search for the new, a new paradigm appears to be growing. Given the complexity and subtlety of the writing process, this paradigm shift may be more difficult and perhaps take longer than the Copernican revolution in astronomy, but it is coming into being. And all those who teach composition are participating right now in the revolution.

Notes

1. Robert J. Connors, Lisa Ede, and Andrea A. Lunsford, "The Revival of Rhetoric in America," in *Essays on Classical Rhetoric and Modern Discourse,* ed. Robert J. Connors, Lisa Ede, and Andrea Lunsford (Carbondale: Southern Illinois Univ. Press, 1984), 1.
2. Connors, Ede, and Lunsford, 1–3.
3. Connors, Ede, and Lunsford, 5–7.
4. William E. Tanner and J. Dean Bishop, "Reform Amid the Revival of Rhetoric," in *Rhetoric and Change,* ed. William E. Tanner and J. Dean Bishop (Mesquite, Tex.: Ide House, 1982), 4–5.
5. Albert R. Kitzhaber, *Themes, Theories, and Therapy: The Teaching of Writing in College,* the Report of the Dartmouth Study of Student Writing (New York: McGraw-Hill, 1963), 26.
6. Kitzhaber, 16.
7. David Foster, *A Primer for Writing Teachers* (Upper Montclair, N.J.: Boynton/Cook, 1983), 17–18.
8. Foster, 34.
9. Foster, 37–39.
10. Foster, 47.
11. Erika Lindemann, *A Rhetoric for Writing Teachers* (New York: Oxford Univ. Press, 1982), 50.
12. Lindemann, 120.
13. Foster, 665.
14. Lindemann, 125.
15. This address was later published: Paul T. Bryant, "A Brand New World Every Morning," *College Composition and Communication* 25 (1974): 30–33.
16. Foster, 25.
17. Gregory Cowan and Elizabeth Cowan, *Writing* (New York: Wiley, 1980), 8–47; and Richard Larson, "Discovery through Questioning: A Plan for Teaching Rhetorical Invention," *College English* 30 (1968): 126–34.
18. Foster, 4.
19. Foster, 10–12.

20. James Britton, Tony Burgess, Nancy Martin, Alex McLeod, and Harold Rosen, *The Development of Writing Abilities (11–18)* (London: Macmillan Education, 1975); Janet Emig, *The Composing Processes of Twelfth Graders,* NCTE Research Report No. 13 (Urbana, Ill.: National Council of Teachers of English, 1971).
21. Janet Emig, "Writing as a Mode of Learning," *College Composition and Communication* 28 (1977): 122–28.
22. For some of these studies, see: Jerome Bruner, R. P. Oliver, and P. M. Greenfield, *Studies in Cognitive Growth* (New York: John Wiley and Sons, 1966); Jean Piaget, *Six Psychological Studies* (New York: Random House, 1967); Jeremy M. Anglin, ed., *Beyond the Information Given: Studies in the Psychology of Knowing* (New York: Norton, 1973); Andrea A. Lunsford, "Cognitive Development and the Basic Writer," *College English* 41 (1979): 38–46. Good general presentations for teachers may be found in Barbara E. Fassler Walvoord, *Helping Students Write Well: A Guide for Teachers in All Disciplines* (New York: Modern Language Association, 1982); and in Karen Burke LeFevre and Mary Jane Dickerson, *Until I See What I Say: Teaching Writing in All Disciplines* (Burlington, Vt.: IDC Publications, 1981).
23. Richard Lloyd-Jones, "Focus and Resolution," in *The Writing Teacher's Sourcebook,* ed. Gary Tate and Edward P. J. Corbett (New York: Oxford Univ. Press, 1981), 33.
24. Maxine Hairston, "The Winds of Change: Thomas Kuhn and the Revolution in the Teaching of Writing," *College Composition and Communication* 33 (1982): 86.

4 Oral Communication

Donald Rubin

As it has evolved in American public schools, at least since NCTE's beginnings in 1911, the teaching of oral communication encompasses a wonderful diversity of subjects and skills. It has included a characteristic emphasis on formal public speaking but also such activities as small-group decision making and discussion, telephone conversation, debate, oral interpretation of literature, dramatic improvisation, theater production in its various phases, broadcast production in its various phases, informational listening, empathic listening, and listening for aesthetic appreciation. Oral communication instruction trains students to analyze their audiences, to organize material according to the purpose for which they are communicating, to accommodate their linguistic style as appropriate to the situation, to use vocal and gestural expression to enhance their messages, to invent and select subject matter, to discern and evaluate patterns of logic, to illustrate, to refute, to self-disclose, and a great deal more.

Cutting across these diverse considerations and unifying them is the *rhetorical tradition.* Contrasting with (but complementary to) some other approaches to communication like grammar study or literary criticism, rhetoric focuses on the *effects* of communication acts on audiences. In the rhetorical tradition, the key to a communicator's effectiveness is the ability to understand the nature of an interaction (e.g., relationships between speaker and audience, the significance of the topic, the purpose for communication) and to *adapt* appropriately.

The term "rhetoric" is now enjoying a revival. In most quarters, though, rhetoric still bears a suspect reputation as the art of deception. In newspaper columns and political speeches, and in common parlance, rhetoric is tainted by association with modifiers like "empty" and "mere." But it wasn't always so. In classical education, rhetoric was the art for which grammar and logic were "merely" prerequisites.

Teachers of speaking and listening have always been proud to be the keepers of the rhetorical tradition. We seek to cultivate in our students a repertoire of styles and strategies. We help them develop a sensitivity to situations that enables them to select the most appropriate style for their various communication tasks.

Of the four language arts—reading, writing, speaking, and listening—there is little doubt that the two oral modalities are the most often used, both in school and out. Yet they receive the least attention in curricula. The reasons for their neglect are many, ranging from educators' skepticism about the need for deliberate instruction in oral communication ("They'll pick it up on their own, won't they?") to the pervasive influence of textbook publishing (effective communication instruction is experiential and does not really lend itself to textbook formulation). But speaking and listening instruction are clearly central to what ought to be going on in English and language arts classes.

Appropriately, then, the trend in English education is toward a concerted effort to provide instruction in oral communication. The rhetorical tradition offers neither a dictionary definition nor a set of objectives but, rather, a philosophical stance and purpose for guiding that instruction.

Artifice and Responsibility

Because the roots of contemporary instruction in oral communication remain so closely connected with the classical rhetorical tradition, it is fitting to turn to ancient Greece for insight into one of the most persistent controversies in speech education. Socrates, as depicted in Plato's *Dialogues,* passionately opposed the practice of sophistry. The Sophists were early speech teachers who earned their wages tutoring the children of well-heeled Athenians in such matters as vocal production and enunciation, argumentation, and figurative language. These skills were much in demand, for it was through pleasing and convincing speech that the paths to political, economic, and social power were open to young Greeks of a certain class—a situation largely unchanged in our own times.

Socrates was distressed by the Sophists because he felt they inculcated in the younger generation a fixation on pretty words. The great philosopher, in contrast, wanted to instill a commitment to truth. The kind of talk taught by the Sophists, he felt, could obfuscate truth. What was more, that kind of talk was particularly dangerous for society because it could be very potent in seducing people's hearts and minds, and yet it was not trained to the service of any higher ideal. (Incidentally, his opinion of that new-fangled invention, writing, was not much higher.)

A couple of millenia later, in the early years of the twentieth century, the "elocutionist movement" committed some of the same alleged sins as the Sophists and was similarly indicted. The elocutionists were speech teachers, and many also supported themselves by giving public performances. Elocutionists specialized in cultivating a dramatic style of vocal delivery through voice training. They even provided instruction in applied nonverbal communication by showing students how to posture and gesture when speaking. The elocutionists practiced a kind of speech pedagogy that educated the mouth, but not the mind. They were disavowed by teachers of rhetoric and communication, who felt that technique ought to follow from meaning-making, not supplant it. It was partly as a response to the elocutionist movement that in 1914 a caucus of teachers formed the American Association of Academic Teachers of Public Speaking, the forerunner of today's Speech Communication Association.

Concerns about focusing unduly on communication techniques were once again aroused during World War II and in the fifties, when communication researchers began to concentrate on factors in persuasion such as the credibility of sources and, especially, propaganda techniques. The research indicated that the way a message is packaged exerts more influence on an audience than the substance of the message. Listeners are strongly affected by all sorts of variables and appeals that, in fact, short-circuit their abilities to evaluate messages critically. Studies of propaganda techniques like the "bandwagon" and "glittering generalities" quickly became a part of speech curricula. Teachers were once again confronted with difficult decisions about how to provide students with some broader perspective about these powerfully persuasive tools.

When instruction does become dominated by an emphasis on performance skills, students get the idea that technique is all that is important about communication. One dangerous consequence is that students will employ these techniques effectively in the service of bad motives. Another danger, ultimately more serious, is that students will never learn that speech is a vehicle dedicated to discovering the merit in ideas, to projecting and defining one's personality and identity, to building bridges that reach out and create a sense of belonging with others. They will confuse artifice with skill. As a result they will never develop real communication skill, but will execute classroom speaking assignments in a perfunctory, formulaic way and express little of their own perspectives and values. And the more promising of them may become cynical.

Many teachers recognize that they cannot teach communication as technique alone. They must also teach responsible communication. In teaching about propaganda techniques, for example, the lesson is often couched as an exercise in consumer protection. ("These are methods that *they* will use against an unwary and uninformed *you*.") The listener is to be on guard against propaganda. Also, high school textbooks typically include an obligatory section on the role of speech in maintaining a democratic society, e.g., that each citizen has an obligation to voice his or her concerns. Finally, it is often in the speech class that students begin to understand why English teachers make such a great fuss about attributing ideas to sources and about the dangers of plagiarism.

These are important lessons about responsibility in communication. But more fundamental are lessons that help students see that they are responsible for *owning* their messages. Students own their messages

1. when they express something about which they care;
2. when they can anticipate that they will contribute to some constructive outcome;
3. when their words are intended to be heard and not just uttered;
4. when they put more work into making them intelligible than listeners must put into deciphering them; and
5. when they regard them as unique expressions of their individuality, expressions that could not have stated just those ideas or in just that way had they issued from someone else's lips.

Teachers help students acquire a sense of responsibility about communicating by insisting that they own their messages (or as listeners, that they respect others' ownership). This is accomplished not through a series of lectures on ethical communication, but over the long run by demonstration and by expectation.

One final point about speech performance and responsibility is crucial in our multicultural society. Questions of language variation cannot be considered apart from attendant issues of politics, economics, and values. For this reason, few educational conundrums have engendered more partisan responses. For the elocutionists, the issue was easily resolved; their job was to teach a genteel style of speech, to eradicate any evidence of social or regional "backwardness." For individuals pursuing certain career paths, broadcasting for example, such a policy may continue to make some sense. By the mid-1960s, however, speech therapy as a profession had rejected a view of nonstandard dialect as a speech pathology.

Today, bidialectalism and bilingualism are regarded as the educational policies of choice. That is, speakers of nonstandard language varieties should retain their native speech patterns for intimate interactions within their home communities, but for interaction in the broader world, they should acquire standard English as a second linguistic code.

In practice, American schools have not been notably successful in imparting bilingualism and bidialectalism. One reason is that we have approached this effort much as we have approached teaching grammar: as an exercise in conveying certain technical information (e.g., subject-verb agreement). The alternative approach, unfortunately less widely used, stresses flexibility in speech styles. In this communicative approach, teachers can build upon students' style-shifting intuitions by creating role-playing scenarios in which students practice interacting with increasingly unfamiliar and distant audiences.

Another reason, nevertheless, that even our best efforts to encourage standard English as a second language variety often fail is the impact of cultural attitudes. One's language variety is intimately bound up with one's sense of cultural identity. Although we can assure students that we respect their cultural roots, those assurances often ring empty. Why, after all, would only the nonstandard speakers need to learn a second language variety if their native speech patterns really were acceptable? And how can these students learn a language variety that represents the dominant culture until and unless they find some way to embrace the values and history of that culture? Indeed, in working with nonstandard speech patterns, the teacher really has little need to deal in technique. The more significant issue lies in helping students discover how they can own their messages, how they can speak in their own voices, within more than one speech style.

Integrity and Integration

The quest for integration among the language arts is reminiscent of the alchemists' search for the philosopher's stone. No one could argue with the goals of integrating language arts: to provide a rich and varied language environment, to reinforce each of the language modalities, to explore in depth themes and topics often emerging from students' own experiences. But like the philosopher's stone, integrating language arts instruction has proved to be an elusive goal. No one is quite certain how to mix the ingredients.

Calls for integration predominate at the elementary level, where it is apparent that students bring to schooling a mine of rich resources in oral communication. Yet the reality of most (certainly not all) elementary curricula diverges in significant ways from the ideals of integration. Reading instruction dominates. What most often falls under the rubric of "language arts" is a mixture of instruction in writing mechanics (punctuation, letter-writing formats), word study (prefixes, suffixes, dictionary skills), and creative writing (whatever that is).

Specific instruction in oral communication, when it appears at all in elementary schools, generally appears in the service of written literacy. (Show-and-tell is perhaps the one common activity that focuses upon oral communication as something other than an incidental means toward promoting literacy.) The language experience approach encourages children to tell stories aloud; teachers transcribe the stories so that the transcriptions can become texts for early reading experiences. Or children take turns reading aloud in reading circles, and teachers use this activity as a check on students' decoding skills. Children may also engage in listening exercises which are often tied to prereading instruction and may be designed to test word-recognition and phoneme-discrimination skills.

Language arts curricula which use oral activities primarily as a means of promoting literacy are only quasi-integrated. Children need instruction that will help them extend the speech registers over which they have mastery. In particular, they will typically have little experience in the more formal registers of speech, which presume little shared background, greater psychological distance, between speaker and listener. The formal registers require language that is explicit, elaborated, and cohesive. This *decontextualized* talk is not only the language that will best prepare students for what they will encounter in written discourse, but also "school talk," the speech that will allow for effective communication throughout students' school careers.

In secondary schools, the English curriculum is traditionally conceived as tripartite: language, literature, and composition. The language portion of this curriculum usually is realized as grammar study, usage, and writing mechanics. The literature curriculum is most often a study of major literary forms and periods. In the past there has been little composition instruction at all—with that little focusing on outlining, research, and copy editing. That leaves little provision for speaking and listening instruction in the English class. An oral book report, a scene or two of *Under Milkwood* rendered orally, a commercial recording of "The Tell-Tale Heart"—these are injected as treats or fillers to break up the class routine.

Many high schools offer an elective course in speech, apart from regular English, sometimes listed as a fine arts class. The typical high school speech class is a speech-a-week survey: the demonstration speech, the speech to actuate, the speech to convince, the informative speech, the speech of introduction, and, if time permits, the oral interpretation and the debate. This course likewise has little room for establishing meaningful links with what goes on in the rest of the English curriculum.

In sum, the ideal of integration in English/language arts instruction has not been widely realized. For the most part, instruction in speaking and listening at both elementary and secondary levels is either conceived as a precursor to reading and writing, or else it is interspersed as leavening in a curriculum dense with more serious pursuits. It is true that the general state of the art in language arts integration is improving. But given the normative treatment of speaking and listening in quasi-integrated instruction, it is little wonder that those in the field of oral communication have sometimes been ambivalent about integrating away its distinct identity and merging it with the broader curriculum in English and language arts.

The kernel of a scheme to reconcile these conflicting positions—the reasonableness of integration among the language arts as opposed to the need to maintain the integrity and visibility of speaking and listening—does exist. It was articulated most prominently in the proceedings of the 1966 Anglo-American Seminar on the Teaching of English, the Dartmouth Conference. For the participants in that conference, instruction in English and language arts must capitalize upon and extend naturalistic processes of language development. Talk and drama thus assume central, not just supporting, roles in the curriculum. They are regarded as tools for academic attainment, much as writing is regarded by the current writing-across-the-curriculum movement. At the same time, proficiency in oral communication is valued equally with proficiency in written literacy, development of a self-concept, and assimilation of a cultural heritage. Dartmouth conferees, incidentally, were quite deliberate in their choices of the terms "talk" rather than "speech" and "drama" rather than "dramatics." Talk is pervasive in the learning community and in everyday life, whereas speech is reserved for more formal occasions and is more consciously contrived. Similarly, drama is simply the enactment of ideas using all communicative means available (gesture, vocal expression, movement). Drama includes theatrical production, but encompasses a broader variety of learning experiences as well.

The solution—to elevate oral communication to a status equal to that of reading and writing—appears simple, but implementing such a solution is not. For us to raise our consciousness with respect to oral communication will require us to train ourselves with a new vocabulary for perceiving and talking about talk. It will require us to be a little less dependent on our textbooks and teacher manuals. Instead, we will need to think about our students' language and interactions as the text from which we teach. These kinds of efforts are, fortunately, supported by our growing understanding of the classroom as a sociolinguistic environment. Teachers inspired by the methods of field-based ethnographic observation can readily appreciate and nurture the value of talk in their own classrooms.

Another tool for elevating the status of speaking and listening in classroom instruction is, admittedly, more manipulative. Assessment programs have always been powerful forces in bringing about curricular change. Experience with some current programs which mandate assessments of students' speaking and listening skills confirms that pattern. When these assessments carefully reflect the rhetorical aims of communication education, and when the assessments are carefully linked to sound curricula, they can indeed serve as the impetus for positive innovations.

Interpersonal and Public

The Dartmouth Conference debate posing *talk* against *speech* parallels the issues raised by teachers about the relative emphasis to be placed on interpersonal communication as opposed to public communication. Classical rhetoric arose to help speakers communicate better with decision-making bodies like legislatures or courts of law. In the nineteenth century, British and American preachers made the greatest contributions to updating and further codifying these principles of rhetoric. One-to-one or one-to-few communication was for many years considered outside the proper scope of formal schooling. Up until the middle of the twentieth century, the major sources of information and guidance about interpersonal communication were chapters on "the art of conversation" in etiquette handbooks.

As a result, the dominance of a public communication emphasis in speech instruction was unchallenged. Students might study the works of great orators—and this was consistent with the emphasis on recitation in English class as well as in other subjects—or engage in much declamation of poetry and prose as part of their coursework in literature or civics. While these kinds of formal speech assignments no longer enjoy much currency (except perhaps for some choral reading in the elementary grades), they have been replaced for the most part with other types of one-to-many speech assignments. In English and language arts classes students deliver oral reports, especially oral book reports. In classes focusing specifically on speech, they learn to give speeches (really "extended monologues," because a speech requires an audience, and not all classrooms make provision for students to take on the role of audience) and perhaps also learn about formal discussion techniques like forums, symposia, and parliamentary procedure. Listening instruction teaches students to comprehend and recall oral messages delivered in lecture format.

In the early 1960s, a Speech Association of America task force on evaluating the high school speech curriculum enumerated the kinds of public communication experiences to which students ought to be exposed. But less than a decade later, a successor committee would make powerful arguments for expanding the scope of speech instruction to include the study of interpersonal relations, the roles of perception and values, leaderless group discussion, and the like. Communication theorists began to augment classical approaches to human discourse with approaches derived from information and general systems theory. They began to think of communication as a process and introduced terms like "feedback" that suggested a circular flow of messages instead of the one-way flow implied by classical rhetoric. At the same time, communication scholars became aware of important work derived from clinical psychology. Psychologists like Carl Rogers regarded interpersonal communication as the key to personal adjustment and directed our attention to skills like empathic listening and "perception checking." The general societal trend likewise seemed to be shifting toward an emphasis on relationship. The popular press marketed a literature promising to improve the quality of one's life, not by increasing one's word power or by increasing one's buying power, but by increasing the honesty and intimacy of one's interpersonal commitments. In the business community new theories of management described how worker morale, and hence worker productivity, could be improved by opening two-way channels of communication. And in teaching, student self-knowledge became a central objective and interaction in the classroom a desirable teaching technique.

Interpersonal communication has rapidly permeated the curriculum. Sometimes it appears under the guise of values clarification in social studies. Sometimes it shows up as units on personal development taught by guidance personnel rather than language arts instructors. In the communication curriculum itself, the interpersonal communication movement is manifest in units on nonverbal communication, on the role of communication in achieving personal satisfaction, on perception and semantics as potential sources of communication breakdown, and on message analysis systems such as transactional analysis. Classroom activities are likely to include a good many small-group problem-solving tasks, personal inventories of communication behaviors and attitudes, role-playing improvisations, and simulation games. Even when curricula do not explicitly acknowledge interpersonal communication objectives, the influence of this trend is evident in activities addressing topics like interviewing, giving and following directions, and cooperation in groups.

The most recent thought in communication pedagogy, however, transcends the division between public and interpersonal communication. Instead, it recognizes the essential unity of communication principles applied in all communication situations. Thus, for example, the rhetorical perspective extends to one-to-one communications. What we talk about as "audience analysis" in public speaking is really not that different from "empathy" or "interpersonal sensitivity" in dyadic conversation. When we teach about forms of support in public speaking, we tell students about the power of anecdote and illustration. In the same vein, we help students see the value of personal narrative in everyday interactions. And when we inculcate a sense of responsibility in public speaking, we help students see the need to project their personalities into their speeches just as they do in their conversations.

Curriculum which is structured by *functions of communication* likewise builds upon the unity of communication principles across interpersonal and public situations. Instruction in "functional communication competence," promoted by a series of publications and committee efforts sponsored in the late seventies by the Speech Communication Association, is organized around such pervasive functions of communication as controlling, describing, imagining, expressing feelings, and ritualizing. Instruction in oral communication is directed toward helping students expand their repertoires of communication behaviors for accomplishing these functions. Thus, for example, a unit on the controlling function might include role-playing activities related to peer or parent-child interaction. It would also demonstrate the effects of pressures toward conformity in small-group settings. It might include work on individual speeches to persuade. And it might provide opportunities for students to learn about persuasive campaigns carried out over mass media.

The conflicts described certainly do not exhaust the kinds of debates that have centered on the teaching of oral communication. Many of the questions—How should nonstandard dialects be treated? What standards ought to be used for selecting literature for children? What is the best balance between practicing communication skills and learning course content about communication?—are identical to the questions facing all of English and language arts education. There is one unique contribution that the study of oral communication can offer to educators facing these difficult questions: the conviction that *conflict is not something to be avoided; it is through conflict that we progress.* Conflict is not a sign of disorder in a profession. Rather, it is a sign of vitality and cohesiveness. Judging from the kinds of conflicts we have experienced thus far in our history, our profession is a healthy community of educators indeed.

II Conditions: Context for Teaching

5 The English Curriculum Today

Ouida Clapp

It holds true for the National Council of Teachers of English in its seventy-fifth anniversary year that "Reading maketh a full man, conference a ready man, and writing an exact man." Although we may be tempted to change "man" to "person" in Francis Bacon's four-hundred-year-old pronouncement, we can still recognize in it the substance of the English curriculum: reading, writing, listening, and speaking—or, to put the skills into a broader context, language, literature, and composition. That substance does not change. Its constancy is unshaken by the century's amazing advances in technology, as writers compose with ease and grace on word processors, as readers call up information from vast memory banks of computers, and as conference proceeds instantaneously between speakers on planet Earth and speakers in the distant reaches of space.

What is the "state of the art" in 1986? The substance of the English curriculum is unchanging, but a healthy variety of content, new approaches, and decisions about goals is omnipresent. The intensity of the dialogue and the fervor of research persist, waxing and waning with the types and the times: What is the appropriate position of the college English department on the structure and content of a writing program across the curriculum? What place does the study of media phenomena like the "docudrama" deserve in the English classroom? Shall we tolerate having instruction in writing the business letter, an item on many states' competency tests, demand as much attention as instruction in writing summaries? On such questions teachers strive for agreements in college and secondary school departments and at professional meetings; in some districts and states elementary and secondary teachers play increasingly important roles in the formulation of district and state education department policy.

No National Curriculum

Historically, the Commission on the English Curriculum of the National Council of Teachers of English has seen greatest merit in curriculum by consensus. It has preferred to examine and describe that consensus rather than undertake the writing of a national curriculum or national guidelines. The five volumes of *The English Language Arts,* prepared by the Commission during the late 1940s and early 1950s, offer a compendium of options. Though the series made strong proposals about such matters as, for example, the need for incorporating an extensive study of mass media into the curriculum, *The English Language Arts* was never intended or viewed as a national curriculum. Dora V. Smith, first director of the Commission, said in the preface to volume 1,

> In the face of the ever-present criticism of the teaching of English—now because it is too traditional, too hidebound, and too intent on narrow skills, and again, because it attends too little to the three R's and too much to fads and fancies—the National Council of Teachers of English appointed in 1945 a Commission on the English Curriculum to study the place of the language arts in life today, to examine the needs and methods of learning for children and youth, and to prepare a series of volumes on the English curriculum. . . .
>
> No organization, though national in scope, can presume to present a curriculum for the schools of the nation. . . . This volume offers a plan for making a curriculum which has proved useful to those working on this study. It presents the evidence of research and the pooled judgment of many of the ablest thinkers in the country who have wrestled with the problems of curriculum-making in English, and it describes practices which have proved successful in schools throughout the nation.[1]

Pinpointing the views of the profession in 1965, the Commission on English of the College Entrance Examination Board, in its landmark report *Freedom and Discipline in English,* discussed the idea of a national curriculum, saying:

> Who can claim the authority to draw up such a master list of literary works specified to be taught to every student? Or to require it, once drawn . . . ? Such a curriculum, prepared by highly competent people, would protect the study of literature from the ephemeral, the merely fashionable, and the patently trivial. It would make possible a sequence in which each year's study would lead clearly to the next. . . . On the other hand a national curriculum . . . implies highly centralized control of education. . . . Whatever advisory or research help may come from the federal government, the responsibility and the control lie elsewhere. That alone makes talk of a national curriculum rather empty. And other counterarguments readily appear . . . national curriculums tend to stifle experimentation, limit inventiveness, and hinder, if they do not actually prevent, adaptation to local needs. . . .[2]

NCTE's 1965–66 Commission on the English Curriculum published *Ends and Issues—1965–66* to speak to what it termed "the confusion" about the English curriculum "arising out of a massive movement to reshape American education." Rather than define English, the Commission decided to have its publication review the field, spotlighting and discussing "the disputes about purpose and program. In this way [it felt it] might also be able to delineate whatever certainties [it might] still wish to claim as a general professional base for intelligent participation in the process of resolving contention." "The call for unity," the Commission asserted, "is almost surely premature.... To make good use of what is now available in curriculum planning, teachers of English need many opportunities to clarify their present sense of purpose, review their convictions about what they believe most needs to be learned, and examine with care the relevance of the content they are choosing or will be urged to choose."[3]

As recently as the 1977 Business Meeting of the National Council of Teachers of English, a charge was given the Commission on the English Curriculum to write national "guidelines for curricula in English similar to the Bullock Report of England." The Commission's response was its 1980 book *Three Language-Arts Curriculum Models: Pre-Kindergarten through College,* a work the Commission's director/editor Barrett J. Mandel described as a radical interpretation of the charge. Said Mandel:

> It soon became evident that those involved with the planning of this publication could not see themselves defining national guidelines in a prescriptive manner. The state of the art in curriculum ... is uncertain and evolving.... If we were to address ourselves to the issue of a national curriculum for the eighties, the focus would have to be on a catholic collection of curriculum models that had been found effective in various regional and educational contexts. "National guidelines" was therefore loosely interpreted to mean "the best of what is happening" rather than "what ought to happen."[4]

The state of the art, described as chaotic in the forties and fifties, "confusing" in 1966, and "evolving and uncertain" in 1980, can be characterized in 1986 as all of the above. The mid-century chaos gave witness to the battle joined around problems of packaging the core curriculum one way for college preparatory students and another for the non–college-bound, and around core curriculum versus life adjustment, or experience education, for all students. What Arthur Applebee called the "academic model"[5] assumed its rigorous shape: classic literature, prescriptive grammar, and formal composition. In the mid-sixties confusion, the elective curriculum swept through the nation's schools, challenging convention with student-teacher choices. At the same time, attention to human concerns in English teaching reached a peak at the Anglo-American Seminar at Dartmouth. During the decade of the seventies a back-to-basics, competency-driven urgency clashed with chastened reconceptualizations of the failed elective curriculum, the latter continuing to champion the student as central to the learning process.

However, where there is chaos it pertains more to structure than to substance. While there is still confusion, there is a stronger, wider-than-ever network of support and assistance for the teacher—from the college, from the inservice programs established in public and private schools and school districts, and from professional organizations on local, state, and national levels. And as the curriculum evolves, English teachers have been able to assume an air of confidence about uncertainty. They realize that the measure of uncertainty inherent in open-mindedness does not ask for abandonment of principle.

Three Distinct Trends

Using the 1980 Commission's working definition of curriculum, "goals, contents, and teaching-learning procedures," today's English teacher can realize how interrelated and interdependent those three elements are. As the 1980 Commission surveyed procedures across the nation, they saw distinct organizational trends emerging in English classroom practice. The Commission decided that these trends moved in three general directions.

They saw a "mastery" orientation that took its cue from performance-based concepts introduced by the behaviorists. "Competency," "pre- and post-testing," and "teacher-student accountability" are terms closely associated with this trend. Another trend identified by the Commission is a "process" orientation, which places great emphasis on the total learning experience of the student and assumes that the acquiring of skills will develop within that framework. Student-centered, human growth, and development concepts determine the treatment of content in a classroom guided by "process" thinking. Third, the Commission found what it called "heritage" undergirding the instruction in numerous English classrooms. Teachers preferring a heritage approach, in the words of the Commission, acknowledge and endorse "traditions, history, the time-honored values of civilized thought and feeling (including the time-honored resistance to these values) and the skills that make it possible to share in one's culture and to pass it on."[6]

The Commission discovered adherents to these three positions at every level of the curriculum, pre-kindergarten through college. However, a careful reading of *Three Language-Arts Curriculum Models,* a delineation of each of the three models at each level, leads to an important conclusion about the English curriculum: that operating in each teaching-learning mode is a centering sense that pulls the procedure to a position recognizing the need for attention to both cognitive and affective development, the desirability of respect for tradition as well as reform, and the significance of the fact that parts belong to wholes. The indication is that one will not find a completely process-, completely competency-, or completely heritage-ordered classroom. Further, each of these models complements the others, suggesting that an eclectic stance serves an English teacher well. Must considerations of competency not enter into the treatment of active and passive voice in a seventh-grade process setting? Or will not a competency teacher at the college level make decisions about process in teaching *Arms and the Man* or *The Color Purple*? What operates out there in the classrooms is the good sense of the English professional, whose curricular choices—whether directed by concerns about tradition, competency, or process—owe their legitimacy to a consensus welded by the research and the practice of past years.

Revolution in Writing

A word must be said about the revolution in writing instruction which has affected the English curriculum more profoundly than any practice, procedure, or recent innovation. Early elementary school teachers are beginning to understand that children can write before they learn to spell words correctly, and that this is good. Teachers at all levels are valuing a composing process that begins with an emphasis on the writer's ideas and the ideas he or she spends time generating, a process that helps the writer to perceive the reader-audience clearly and to hold the purpose for writing firmly in mind. The revolution has given new life to listening and speaking in their role as prewriting activities and as techniques to be refined during peer-assisted revision. Reading is experiencing a reexamination as a language art, a mirror image, perhaps, of writing, employing the same thinking processes. Such interest spawns innumerable studies, articles, and conference presentations with topics like "Writing to Read" and "The Reading-Writing Connection." And writing possesses a life of its own, independent now of its use in responding to literature. Writing centers, firmly established on both two- and four-year college campuses, espouse a doctrine of collaborative learning, writer with tutor and peers. Where a college curriculum might once have depended on freshman composition to solve writing problems, it will now offer an ample menu of courses to support the developing writer's needs: Writing for Careers, Practical Writing, Essay and Article Writing, Public Relations Writing, Writing Poetry, Writing Exposition. Further, teacher training programs now prepare teachers to teach writing. Courses named Teaching Writing, Teaching Fiction Writing, Teaching Writing in the Elementary and Secondary Schools, Teaching Poetry Writing, and even the History and Teaching of Writing are routine.

The times create, as always, populations whose needs claim particular attention. English teachers seek and design methods and materials for academically talented, linguistically diverse, and nontraditional students, as well as the offspring of today's media ecology. Through it all in the classroom, the teacher's private domain, a dynamic set of dualities exists, auguring well for the future of the curriculum: Self-realization is a primary goal for teachers and for students, while at the same time teachers and students work together to forge effective public identities for students. To achieve this, after surveying the curricular procedures which they and their colleagues deem laudable, teachers choose those goals, contents, and procedures that are most in harmony with the pursuit of personal fulfillment. In the process, the curriculum renews itself and thrives.

Notes

1. Commission on the English Curriculum of the National Council of Teachers of English, *The English Language Arts* (New York: Appleton-Century-Crofts, 1952), 1:vii, ix.
2. Commission on English of the College Entrance Examination Board, *Freedom and Discipline in English* (Princeton, N. J.: College Entrance Examination Board, 1965), 42, 43.
3. Alexander Frazier, ed., and the Commission on the English Curriculum of the National Council of Teachers of English, *Ends and Issues—1965–66: Points of Decision in the Development of the English Curriculum* (Champaign, Ill.: National Council of Teachers of English, 1966), 1, 2.
4. Barrett J. Mandel, ed., *Three Language-Arts Curriculum Models: Pre-Kindergarten through College* (Urbana, Ill.: National Council of Teachers of English, 1980), 1, 2.
5. Arthur N. Applebee, *Tradition and Reform in the Teaching of English: A History* (Urbana, Ill.: National Council of Teachers of English, 1974), 185.
6. Mandel, 8.

6 Teacher Education

Theodore Hipple

In all likelihood the debate began early on. A caveman threw a rock at a charging saber-toothed tiger and frightened it away. With a flash of insight the caveman realized that here was a protective strategy that the youngsters in the cave needed to know. So that night at the council campfire was initiated the first discussion in the content/methodology controversy that has plagued teacher education ever since: Should the person who teaches rock throwing to the young be an expert rock thrower or an expert teacher of rock throwing? Even in those unenlightened times the elders realized the difficulty of trying to find someone acceptable to both camps, a good rock thrower and a good teacher of rock throwing.

Probably this issue of content versus pedagogy will never be resolved to everyone's satisfaction. It will remain an open question, like many of those which have marked the distant and recent history of teacher education. In its own seventy-five years NCTE has been both an active force and a highly interested spectator in the bloodless but nonetheless impassioned battles about preparing prospective and practicing teachers. NCTE has always attempted to inform its members and friends of what the issues were, a practice it continues with volumes like this one.

Today most teachers are trained at the university or college level, where the curriculum they study may best be seen as a compromise generated, not always happily, by several different groups who demand certain courses and experiences for teachers. Colleges of education argue for courses in methods of teaching English and for related course work in educational philosophy, adolescent psychology, learning theory, tests and measurement, and classroom management, with a strong field experience component that culminates in an extended period of internship. English departments want teachers to be steeped in all the major areas of English, American, and world literature, with newcomers like women's literature and ethnic literature recently added to the mix; in composition, both new and old rhetorics, including considerable attention to writing as process;

and in language, with knowledge of at least two grammars. State certification boards demand a strong general education program for the prospective teachers they are asked to certificate: freshman composition, courses in Western civilization, physical and natural sciences, humanities, math, etc. Additionally, they want English teachers to have not only the aforementioned English and education courses, but also work in speech, drama, and the media. The local school, the ultimate employer and thus an important standard-setter, hopes teachers of English will have a minor field and be able to coach a sport or sponsor the yearbook or direct the junior play. Professional organizations like NCTE enter the debate on occasion, sometimes with documents like the 1986 *Guidelines for the Preparation of Teachers of English Language Arts,* a booklet that can significantly influence preservice and inservice training.

Somehow out of all this turmoil, these occasionally convergent but often conflicting demands, English teachers did and do get trained by their universities and colleges, do go out in the world and get jobs (not always the case; as recently as the mid-seventies, English teachers glutted the market), and do achieve a modicum of success in those jobs. Once there, however, they meet again the same uncertainty that characterized their undergraduate curriculum, though here the rubric is "inservice education."

How much of what is new, and may be voguish and short-lived, should teachers examine on their work days? The answer to this crucial question has never been easy. Transformational/generative grammar proved not to be the panacea some of its late-sixties proponents predicted it would be, yet many teachers spent after-school hours, summer workshop time, even NCTE convention sessions learning how to create tree diagrams that never found a place on their chalkboards back home. The spiral-based school curricula that teachers put together spun their way into obscurity. Initial teaching alphabets succumbed to the staying power of the traditional twenty-six. Elective programs failed at reelection time. Even *Silas Marner,* long a staple of tenth-grade literature, finally reached retirement age and was removed from textbooks, thus taking from American life what amounted to an almost universal reading experience and removing at least one speech from each NCTE convention.

Though the topics change, these same inservice debates continue today: bilingual versus unilingual education (an issue that threatens to become a national political, social, and educational controversy of some magnitude), optimum class size in English classes, especially at the secondary level (NCTE has long argued for four classes for English teachers, with a maximum of one hundred students altogether); testing (classroom-, school-, district-, state-, or nation-based); writing in the elementary grades (where even kindergartners keep journals). Faced with a whole array of reforms, directions, incentives, trends, and movements, few inservice coordinators can plan extended programs with much confidence that what they are suggesting teachers study is indeed the best that could and should be offered to them.

Though particularly germane to English language arts teachers, these kinds of issues must vie for inservice time with such important but more widely applicable matters as merit pay and career ladders and differentiated staffing and burnout; these are potential trouble spots for all teachers, no matter the subject or grade they teach. In sum, then, it remains difficult to get a handle on what inservice programs are, much less on what they should be. The demands of the moment, the items that attract a principal's or supervisor's attention, the dog-and-pony show a visiting consultant is currently pushing, all contend for supremacy in the inservice halls.

Similarly, colleges and universities have been beset by general issues: competency testing; entrance and exit standards for teachers; recruiting and retaining able students in teacher-education programs; how much and what kinds of field experience are necessary; and the optimum length—four or five years—of preservice programs. Sometimes the debates that raged within the college of education between, say, the ed. psych. professors and the elementary education instructors down the hall over where classroom management techniques should be taught were as fierce as those between English-education professors and English instructors over control of the methods course.

Thus the last twenty-five years or so of preservice and inservice teacher training have been marked not so much by consensus arising from dissent as by confusion growing out of necessity. Universities and colleges *had* to require some courses; state certification boards *had* to demand some competencies; schools *had* to have some criteria on which to base their hiring policies and their inservice programs. NCTE's role has been part leader, part follower, part reporter of the ebbs and flows, the pendulum swings. Indeed, slightly over two decades ago, the shifting premises of teacher education called for an NCTE subgroup that would attend to this important subject, and the Conference on English Education was established. CEE and its journal, *English Education,* have been important in the NCTE attempt to address these significant changes in teacher education, preservice and inservice. NCTE's multifaceted performance has been appropriate: When consensus seemed at hand, NCTE spread the word; its support for reduced class size is one example, its promulgation of the

Essentials of English statement another. When disagreement seemed loud and widespread, NCTE did not avoid the fray, but entered more as light-shedder than as torch-bearer; its caution about advocating a single kind of language study comes to mind. Always, the Council has sought to alert its members, subscribers, and convention participants to what is going on. Its journals, special pamphlets, and books, its regional and national convention programs, its affiliate services, its cosponsorship of speakers, have shared common missions: to keep the interested aware, to help the uninformed become knowledgeable, to bring intelligence and insight to the discussion, to stay on the cutting edge.

These are missions that the future may demand as well. Almost no one argues that nirvana is here, that today what English teachers learn in their training programs and what they later gain through inservice programs in their schools is now perfect, purified, agreed upon by all concerned. Rather, the changing priorities of the past decades sustain a prophecy of continuing dissent that will seek to become consensus. The people have changed, the topics have changed, but the debates remain. For example, a contemporary concern focuses on the amount of computer knowledge teachers should have, to what extent they should be "computer literate." How long hence before all ninth-grade themes are produced on word processors, those at home or those at school? Will spelling instruction become a forgotten classroom activity, as students simply insert a "Spell It Correctly" disk and watch the machine change *ocurance* to *occurrence*?

At the university level teacher preparation will continue its uncertain straddling between educating teachers for the schools that are—training them to teach traditional grammar, for instance—and educating them for the schools that, in the opinion of the trainers, ought to be—helping them to use alternative language strategies and tactics as substitutes for grammar, for example. Adding to the uncertainty are practices that may remove the colleges of education from the action altogether, or at least reduce their part in it. Some states have enacted legislation that would permit their certification boards to grant a license to anyone with a bachelor's degree, with no education courses at all; pedagogy can be taken in the evening or during summers, with the amount required greatly reduced. Other states are evaluating on-site training programs, where much of teacher education would take place in elementary or secondary schools; again, there would be a substantial reduction in the usual educational psychology, foundations, and even special methods courses.

Yet at a time when some states are saying that far less coursework in education is needed, others are crying out for more and are opting for extended programs in teacher education, programs that last five or even six years. In addition, universities are wondering whether to warrant their graduates, something they will be unlikely to do if they have not had a major hand in the training those graduates receive. If beginning teacher Smith makes a botch of his or her third-grade class, should Professor Jones be sent out from the university to provide on-site help?

Further, preservice and inservice English teachers have been singled out by the educational reform writers. Ernest Boyer, in *High School,* and John Goodlad, in *A Place Called School,*[1] argue for the supremacy of English language arts in the schools, an awareness that may add both tension and attention to the teaching of the subject, this at a time when many teachers are busy simply keeping alive and coping each day with their 150-plus high school students or their 30-plus elementary ones. Their day-to-day struggles leave them little stomach for outside imperatives, no matter how well intentioned. In a 1985 report that promises to rival the bombastic *Nation at Risk* document of 1983, the National Commission for Excellence in Teacher Education provided sixteen recommendations for improvements in teacher education. These range over a broad but already tilled field—better pay for teachers, high standards for their admission to teacher education programs, more rigor in those programs, greater citizen awareness of teacher education and of teaching—and may well herald a heightened consciousness among the populace; but they may simply muddy already troubled waters.

Goodlad also writes about a basic inconsistency between being an educator and being a pessimist; still, there is less cause for optimism than one would like, and almost none at all for rejoicing. Though it is too much a posture of gloom and doom to predict revolution, it is worth suggesting that the future for English language arts teachers, both newly minted and well seasoned, may be more shrouded in disarray and uncertainty than the past has been. The profession as a whole cannot agree on the answers; sometimes there is even loud debate about what the questions ought to be.

It is at this point that NCTE must continue to play its vital role. With efforts like those spawned by a special Task Force on Centers of Excellence, NCTE can explore the better roads, the higher plains, and perhaps draw others after it. The task force is finding and publicizing a number of demonstration centers where teachers can find excellent programs, even entire schools, that are exemplary and replicable back home. Through its continued help for affiliate networks, NCTE can try to achieve lowered class size, using its lobbying influence, the power of its research base, and its moral support for others engaged in the same kinds of activity.

In sum, then, the debates will go on. So will NCTE. It must provide a forum for discussion and a method of dissemination about the pros and cons of issues affecting English teaching. And what affects teaching also affects teacher education, both preservice and inservice. Whether it is testing or bilingual education, extended teacher education programs or warranties for graduates, even something as basic (and as hoary) as What is English? all can become grist for the NCTE mills. Out of these continuing efforts comes dissent, certainly; consensus, maybe; improved practice, ideally; and greater learning, eventually.

Note

1. John I. Goodlad, *A Place Called School: Prospects for the Future* (New York: McGraw-Hill, 1984); and Ernest L. Boyer, *High School: A Report on Secondary Education in America* (New York: Harper and Row, 1983).

7 The Uses of Research

Allan Glatthorn with Catherine C. Hatala and Beatrice Moore

One of the important questions which the profession in general and the National Council of Teachers of English in particular, in its seventy-five-year history, have addressed is how to help teachers make curricular and instructional decisions that are more informed and insightful. The need seems especially acute now and for the immediate future. Public insistence on the importance of quality education seems to mount in intensity. Researchers continue to generate new knowledge about teaching and learning. And the computer makes it easier to retrieve the kind of information that is useful in making informed decisions. It therefore seems especially appropriate that those responsible for planning this collection of essays saw fit to include a contribution on the English teacher and the uses of research.

Rather than focusing too narrowly on the English teacher as a consumer of research, however, this chapter attempts to provide a more useful contribution by assessing the extent of the problem, analyzing the deficiencies of the conventional response to the problem, and then suggesting several alternative solutions that emerge from that analysis.

The English Teacher's Interest in Research

To what extent are English teachers interested in educational research? The answer is not encouraging to those who have a vision of the teacher as an eager consumer of the latest research findings. First, teachers in general are frequently criticized for ignoring research. After noting that much medical research is disseminated by esteemed practitioners who are the first to apply research findings, R. W. Tyler notes that "the number of persons who are confident of their teaching effectiveness and seek to improve by making use of new knowledge is too small to furnish the major channel for stimulating the use of research by the practitioner."[1] His observation is echoed in the lamentations of less generous critics, who seem to portray the teacher as an unthinking and obdurate technician oblivious to the usefulness of research.

And English teachers seem no different from their colleagues. Consider some evidence. As of February 1985 only thirty-four hundred members of the profession subscribed to *Research in the Teaching of English*. The forty-four thousand who subscribed to the *English Journal* were not likely to find many research-based articles in its current issues: an analysis of five randomly selected issues published in 1984 revealed no reports of primary empirical research and only one review of research—an ERIC review on the uses of adolescent literature. The editors of the journal, who no doubt make decisions about content based upon their perceptions of their audience's interests, seem more inclined to include hortatory articles ("We English teachers must . . . ") and anecdotal reports ("This is how I did it . . ."). And after a year of operation, NCTE's Teacher Researcher program had attracted only seventy-eight applications.[2]

A recent survey of English teachers tends to support this somewhat negative assessment. Clinton Burhans's 1985 survey of English teachers in Michigan revealed that there are no significant differences between experienced teachers and neophytes in their interest in research: both groups in general seemed not informed about current developments in reading, writing, and literature.[3]

The Conventional Solution

Most of those who have addressed the issue seem to have framed the question so narrowly that they offer what appear to be misguided solutions. Their views, perhaps best identified as the "knowledge-production-and-utilization" perspective, might be paraphrased in this way:

> We now have a clearly formulated science of teaching, based upon a reliable body of evidence that can tell teachers how to teach. All we need to do now is find the most effective way of disseminating this knowledge—to make teachers better consumers of research.

A very direct advocacy of this knowledge-production-and-utilization view can be found in an interview with the director of a consortium called PREPS (Program of Research and Evaluation for Public Schools), whose work is cited by the interviewer as "exemplary."[4] The director, a professor of statistics, sees the agricultural extension service as an "operational model" for university–public school cooperation. Just as an extension agent takes information about hybrid seeds to the farmer, who eagerly plants them and sees a dramatic increase in production, so the "delivery system" of the consortium should disseminate new research findings to the waiting teacher, who can apply them and watch achievement increase.

Such a formulation of the problem leads to obvious conclusions: we simply need to improve our "delivery systems" and to find more effective means of persuading recalcitrant teachers. Such conclusions, we would argue, are seriously flawed. And before we propose some alternative responses, it might be useful to understand how they are flawed.

The Nature of Scientific Knowledge

The first and perhaps most basic error in this conventional view is what we consider its misconceptualization of scientific knowledge. As Margret Buchmann so cogently points out,[5] advocates of such a position make two related mistakes here. They begin by according scientific knowledge too much certainty. Even the best knowledge, Buchmann reminds us, is time-bound, theory-dependent, and selective. Perhaps one example here from educational research would be illuminating. Countless articles published in recent years have urged teachers to apply the "soundly established" research finding that increasing time on task will improve achievement.[6] Yet, after critically analyzing all the research on time on task, Nancy Karweit concludes that "by a variety of criteria for the importance of an effect, the most outstanding finding relating to the effects of time-on-task to learning is that the effects are as small as they are."[7]

The other mistake regarding scientific knowledge involves an overemphasis on the utilization of knowledge. Such an overemphasis, Buchmann notes, distorts the nature of knowledge, downplays its fallibility, and suggests that utility is the primary criterion of sound knowledge. F. N. Kerlinger, in fact, argues that the basic purpose of scientific research is theory—theory that leads to understanding and explanation—and points out forcefully that an insistence on "payoff" and "relevance" can lead to a neglect of basic research.[8] Consider here an example in the field of English. An insistence that all linguistic research should have practical utility for the classroom, if taken seriously, would probably eliminate much of the basic research presently being conducted.

The Relationship between the Theoretical and the Practical

This misconstrual of the nature of scientific knowledge is associated with the second weakness in the knowledge-production-and-utilization approach: it simplifies the relationship between the theoretical and the practical, between the researcher's laboratory and the teacher's classroom. The adherents to the knowledge-production-and-utilization paradigm seem to hold a naive view of the relationship that might be summarized in this fashion:

> Theory and practice should be closely linked. Researchers should generate sound theory and develop empirically based findings that can then be disseminated to teachers in the classroom. Followup studies should be conducted to determine to what extent teachers apply that knowledge without distorting it.

Joseph J. Schwab has perhaps been most effective in challenging the basic assumptions undergirding this view, arguing that the theoretical and the practical are radically different in their methods, in the sources of the problems they study, in their subject matters, and in their outcomes.[9] Thus the scholar is concerned with discovering a generalizable and enduring truth; the teacher is concerned with making an effective decision for a set of unique circumstances. The researcher asks, "Does between-draft revision produce a final draft that is qualitatively superior to writing that has not been revised between drafts?" The teacher grading student essays over the weekend asks, "On Monday we start a new unit—is it worth the time and effort to ask Joe to revise this composition?" The other difficulty with this perspective on research and practice is that it views the teacher as a somewhat passive receiver of the truth—a "consumer," in the lexicon of some researchers. Such a view denigrates the role of the teacher and depreciates the practical knowledge of the classroom teacher.

The Complexities of Schools as Organizations

The third difficulty with the knowledge-production-and-utilization approach is that its basic tenets seem insensitive to the complexities of schools as organizations. Too many of those urging the one-way transmission of knowledge from laboratory to classroom seem to think of schools as businesses or factories—rational and orderly organizations led by a manager interested in the latest research and able to mandate change. (Their rallying cry might be translated as, "We can be like McDonald's!") T. Deal notes several important differences in schools as organizations—differences that seriously complicate the utilization of knowledge: educational goals are diverse and diffuse; the relationship between instructional activities and outcomes is problematic; schools are highly sensitive to local politics; schools and classrooms within a district are only loosely connected with one another; evaluations are rarely used to guide decision making; and within the district, school, and classroom, individuals do not agree on important organizational issues. He further notes that efforts to change these patterns have largely been unsuccessful.[10]

The Complexities of Classroom Life

Another serious error made by those advocating the one-way transmission of knowledge is their ignoring the complexities of classroom life. Too often their "research-based" advice seems based upon a simplistic notion of what occurs in classrooms: "If English teachers only understood the importance of peer feedback, they would use peer response groups in their classrooms." Ann Lieberman and Lynne Miller and others who have taken the time to study life in classrooms have a quite different understanding.[11] Most experienced teachers believe that they do understand the relevant research, but they are more concerned with establishing a classroom environment that they can manage with some degree of success. They develop routines and schedules to reduce uncertainty. ("Spelling test on Friday.") They establish rules to prevent disruption in crowded classrooms. ("No talking while you write.") And they choose curriculum content that will fit readily into the "batch-processing" constraints of teaching thirty or more forgetful and unmotivated students in forty-five-minute blocks of time. ("We're going to work on personal pronouns today.") This is not the mindless behavior of the uninformed; it is the practical decision making of those who have learned to cope.

The Nature of Teachers' Thinking

Perhaps the most serious flaw in the knowledge-production-and-utilization approach is that it oversimplifies the nature of teachers' thinking and decision making. Many of the advocates of this approach convey a belief that research knowledge should be the primary determiner of action: if only teachers knew better, they would act more wisely. Donald Schön attacks this simplistic view, which he calls "technical rationality," in this way:

> According to [this model]—the view of professional knowledge which has most powerfully shaped both our thinking about the professions and the institutional relations of research, education, and practice—professional activity consists in instrumental problem solving made rigorous by the application ofscientific theory and technique.[12]

If technical rationality does not sufficiently explain teachers' decision making, then what does? Perhaps the most useful conceptualization is that offered by F. Michael Connelly and Freema Elbaz.[13] They propose on the basis of their research that teachers' decisions grow out of their *personal practical knowledge,* a body of knowledge held in a uniquely practical way, structured in terms of the teacher's practical purposes, and derived from the teacher's lived experiences. This personal practical knowledge, in their analysis, has first of all five related orientations: to the context of specific situations ("What should I do in my fifth-period class tomorrow?"); to various theories of practice ("What does James Moffett suggest?"); to social conditions and constraints ("What does the community think about values clarification?"); to self ("What kind of writing do I value?"); and to experience ("What have I learned about teaching writing to adolescents?"). And the personal practical knowledge is organized at three levels of generality: rules of practice ("Have an activity on the board when the students arrive"); practical principles ("Give students a clearly structured learning environment"); and images ("A good essay is like a well-planned house").

Thus, a particular teaching decision—for example, to have students begin the period by writing a paragraph about their attitude toward terrorism—is the result of the interaction of several forces, and is shaped to only a very limited extent by the bits and pieces of theory and research the teacher happens to remember. It is not especially helpful at such a time to say to the teacher, "You were wrong to assign that paragraph; the experts say that you should not teach paragraphs in isolation." The teacher views the criticism as unfair and insensitive; he or she has heard that advice before, has chosen to ignore it on this particular occasion, and is weary of hearing about "the research" and "the experts." For such teachers, acting with the best of intentions out of their personal practical knowledge, more effective "delivery systems" and more skillful "linkage agents" are not the answer.

More Effective Alternatives

What more useful alternatives are suggested by this analysis? What can the profession do in the years ahead to help the teacher make instructional decisions that are more insightful and informed? Several approaches successfully implemented in recent years seem to hold great promise.

A Different Orientation

We begin with a fresh orientation on the part of researchers. Instead of viewing the classroom only as a place where research findings are applied, the classroom should become, as Connelly and D. J. Clandinin remind us, "the ground for inquiry," the focus of research.[14] There researchers and teachers collaborate in understanding practice for the purpose of refining it. Such a fresh orientation has in fact characterized much of the recent research on the teaching of writing.[15] However, it needs to be extended to other fields of English language arts: we need more classroom-focused studies on the teaching of literature and language. Instead of more tedious pronouncements about why the teaching of grammar is ineffective, we need studies that attempt to understand why teachers continue to teach grammar and which methods seem effective.

The Teacher as Researcher

Rather than seeing the teacher only as a passive consumer of research, several scholars have been implementing programs in which the teacher plays an active role on the research team. Perhaps the best known of such programs is Interactive Research and Development, first developed by B. A. Ward and W. J. Tikunoff in 1975.[16] They identify six salient characteristics of collaborative inquiry: it involves the research consumer; it focuses on the problems of the research consumer; it uses collaborative decision making throughout the research project; it presents professional growth opportunities to participants; it attends concurrently to research and application; and it attends to the complexity and maintains the integrity of the classroom. One noteworthy example of such collaborative inquiry in the field of English language arts is the study on the acquisition of writing literacy reported by C. M. Clark and S. Florio.[17] The research team included six researchers and a two-teacher team in each classroom; and the teacher-researchers played an active role by serving as subjects, collecting data, and participating in the data analysis and synthesis. Clark and Florio note that the active participation of the teachers was instrumental in the conduct of the study.

Increasing such collaborative efforts in the field of English language arts might be more effective than NCTE's current Teacher-Researcher Program, which invites full-time English teachers to conduct classroom-based research and limits awards to $1,000.

A Fresh Approach to Staff Development

At the present time most staff-development programs seem unduly concerned with the linear transmission and translation of knowledge into practice, using consultants who in effect say, "Here's the research on how best to teach—let me explain how you should use it." For example, contributors to the 1983 National Society for the Study of Education yearbook on staff development recommend that those planning the content of staff development for their districts should begin by examining the results of the Beginning Teacher Evaluation Study, a research project conducted in the late 1970s in second- and fifth-grade classrooms.[18]

While there is an obvious need for teachers to be informed about such research, we would achieve much better results by using an approach which Buchmann calls "conversation about teaching," a dialogic encounter of peers. Buchmann describes the tone of such conversation in this fashion:

> In conversation, ideas . . . collide and mingle with one another and are diluted and complicated in the process. The pleasant tone of conversation is inimical to doctrinaire notions. In conversation, one may differ and still not disagree; the defensive, corrective, and didactic aspects of rhetoric are out of place. People do not insist that partners follow, it is enough that they enter into conversation. Thus conversation respects great differences and ranges easily over different provinces of meaning: dreams, play, science, and action.[19]

Thus we might imagine a meeting in which a linguist, a district coordinator, a department chair, a principal, and several English teachers are meeting as peers for conversation about the teaching of grammar. The conversation ranges over such issues as the following:

1. What are some contemporary grammars that might be of interest to teachers? Should some parts of each be used in an eclectic approach?
2. Why do parents seem to insist that traditional grammar be taught?
3. From the teachers' vantage point, what functions does the teaching of grammar serve?
4. What types of research studies on the teaching of grammar have been conducted? How rigorously have these studies been designed and implemented? To what extent can their findings be generalized?
5. What kind of software could be developed that would help students identify the parts of speech? Who would use such software? For what purpose? In what grades?
6. What research studies could be conducted in our own classrooms on the teaching of grammar?

Such dialogue, we believe, would be mutually enlightening for all participants. Note, however, that this dialogue is an active process of exchanging information and sharing views; it is not the aimless discussion that seems to result when a consultant "facilitator" says, "I'm here to learn from you."

A Different View of Teacher Supervision

Although Madeline Hunter herself has denied that she has developed a formula for effective teaching, numerous school administrators and supervisors throughout the country seem to be advocating an approach to supervision based on the assumption that her "template" for effective lessons is in fact a recipe that must be followed ("Where was your anticipatory set?").[20] A. C. Costa, however, points out that, despite her disclaimers, Hunter's and other similarly "scientific" approaches reduce teaching, learning, curriculum, and supervision to their lowest common denominators and ignore the aesthetic bases of such endeavors.[21]

While we believe that beginning teachers can profit from supervision that provides the reassuring structure of Hunter's templates, we hold that experienced teachers—and especially experienced English language arts teachers—could profit from a different kind of supervisory encounter. Such a dialogic encounter would have as its goal helping the teacher recall, reflect about, understand, rethink, and discuss a particular lesson or series of lessons. Here are some of the questions and observations that a supervisor might make in such a dialogic encounter:

1. What do you remember most about that lesson?
2. What were you thinking about when you decided to read that passage?
3. On several occasions you used the metaphor of *stretching*. What does that metaphor mean to you? Why do you think you use it with that class?
4. You seemed to be trying to pace their reading of the novel. Talk a bit about what pacing means to you.
5. Some researchers have talked about the importance of eliciting a personal response to the novel. What are your views on the matter?
6. You ended class by asking them a question. Do you do that often? How do the students respond?

Such questions and observations do not attempt to restrict the teacher's repertoire to a sequence of "scientific" teaching acts; they intend instead to enlighten, expand, and liberate through interactive dialogue.

A Concluding Note

We obviously believe that most English teachers are intelligent and concerned professionals, overloaded with conflicting demands and expectations. We believe as well that they can make more informed instructional decisions if scholars, administrators, and supervisors make a special effort to understand their world.

Notes

1. R. W. Tyler, "Diffusion and Adoption in Educational Practice," in *Using What We Know about Teaching,* ed. P. L. Hosford (Alexandria, Va.: Association for Supervision and Curriculum Development, 1984), 21.
2. We wish to express our thanks to the NCTE staff members who so helpfully supplied us with the above data on subscriptions and research applications.
3. Clinton S. Burhans, Jr., "English Teachers and Professional Reading," *English Education* 17 (1985): 81–85.
4. W. Duckett, "A Collaborative Approach to Research and Evaluation in Mississippi: An Interview with Thomas Saterfiel," *Phi Delta Kappan* 66 (1984): 144–47.
5. Margret Buchmann, "The Use of Research Knowledge in Teacher Education and Teaching," *American Journal of Education* 92 (1984): 421–39.
6. See, for example, D. C. Berliner, "The Half-Full Glass: A Review of Research on Teaching," in *Using What We Know about Teaching,* 51–77.
7. Nancy L. Karweit, *Time on Task: A Research Review* (Baltimore, Md.: Center for Social Organization of Schools, Johns Hopkins University, 1983), 46.
8. F. N. Kerlinger, "The Influence of Research on Educational Practice," *Educational Researcher* 6, no. 8 (1977): 5–12.
9. Joseph J. Schwab, *The Practical: A Language for Curriculum* (Washington, D.C.: National Education Association, 1970).
10. T. Deal, "Linkage and Information Use in Organizations" (Paper presented at the Annual Meeting of the American Educational Research Association, San Francisco, April 1979).
11. Ann Lieberman and Lynne Miller, *Teachers, Their World, and Their Work* (Alexandria Va.: Association for Supervision and Curriculum Development, 1984).
12. Donald A. Schön, *The Reflective Practitioner: How Professionals Think in Action* (New York: Basic Books, 1983), 21.
13. F. Michael Connelly and Freema Elbaz, "Conceptual Bases for Curriculum Thought: A Teacher's Perspective," in *Considered Action for Curriculum Improvement,* ed. A. W. Foshay (Alexandria, Va.: Association for Supervision and Curriculum Development, 1980), 95–119.
14. F. Michael Connelly and D. J. Clandinin, *On Narrative Method, Personal Philosophy, and Narrative Unities in the Study of Teaching* (Paper presented at the Annual Meeting of the National Asociation for Research in Science Teaching, French Lick, Indiana, April 1985).
15. For an excellent review of such research, see D. Holdzkom, L. J. Reed, E. J. Porter, and D. L. Rubin, *Research within Reach: Oral and Written Communication* (St. Louis: CEMREL, 1983).
16. For a current review of their and others' efforts see W. J. Tikunoff and B. A. Ward, "Collaborative Research on Teaching," *Elementary School Journal* 83 (1983): 453–68.
17. C. M. Clark and S. Florio, *Understanding Writing in Schools: A Descriptive Study of Writing and Its Instruction in Two Classrooms—Final Report* (East

Lansing, Mich.: Institute for Research on Teaching, Michigan State University, 1981).

18. See Kenneth R. Howey and Joseph C. Vaughan, "Current Patterns of Staff Development," in *Staff Development,* ed. G. D. Griffin, Eighty-Second Yearbook of the National Society for the Study of Education, part 2 (Chicago: University of Chicago Press, 1983), 92–117.
19. Margret Buchmann, "Improving Education by Talking: Argument or Conversation?" *Teachers College Record* 86 (1985): 449.
20. See Madeline Hunter, "What's Wrong with Madeline Hunter?" *Educational Leadership* 42 (1985): 274–75.
21. A. C. Costa, "A Reaction to Hunter's Knowing, Teaching, and Supervising," in *Using What We Know about Teaching,* 196–204.

8 Tests and the Teaching of English

Enduring Issues in Language Arts Testing

Rexford Brown

Evaluation is at the heart of the learning experience. That, at least, has not changed in the seventy-five-year history of the National Council of Teachers of English. The most important evaluation is the learner's own. Unless a learner feels a sense of accomplishment and improvement, it is hard to imagine why he or she would want to continue learning. One of the ultimate goals of education, then, is to help young people develop and internalize criteria by which to judge themselves and with which they can eventually take charge of their own learning. All other kinds of evaluation in school can contribute to that goal—or frustrate it.

Teachers' evaluations can help students develop clear, consistent, realistic standards, or they can so mystify the whole process of standards that some students come to believe there are none. To such students, grades become someone else's responsibility and reflect someone else's values and desires, not their own. When evaluation is mysterious and cut off from learning—as, for instance, when students receive a grade on a paper but no corrective feedback—learning takes a back seat to "psyching out" the teacher.

Evaluation involves testing, and testing begins with teachers. There are teacher-made tests that are inseparable from the learning experience and teacher-made tests cut off from the learning experience. There are teacher-made tests that teach students, and teacher-made tests that rank them, control them, or punish them. Within the language arts there are teacher-made tests that directly or indirectly assess student competence.

Then there are tests from beyond the classroom. These are either commercial or noncommercial (district, state, or federal). They, too, can be more or less connected to learning, more or less used for ranking; and they, too, may include direct or indirect measures of achievement. By and large, they tend to be disconnected from learning, used primarily for ranking and heavily dependent upon indirect measures.

Seventy-five years ago, when NCTE was born, many people believed that educational advancement was scandalously arbitrary. It appeared as if students passed or failed, gained entrance to prestigious universities or were turned away on nothing more substantial than whims or family connections. Some educators hoped that the fledgling science of mental measurement would establish grounds upon which to make fairer judgments and selections tied only to merit. Commercial testing grew in response to that hope. It flourished as schooling flourished, as mental measurement burgeoned, and as American education became increasingly bureaucratic and centralized.

The issues surrounding testing in America are complex. They have roots in paradoxes and contradictions that lie at the heart of America's cultural, social, and economic history. Since increased testing went hand in hand with increased centralization and bureaucratization, for instance, resistance to standardized testing may be a way of calling for more local autonomy or a return to the simpler structures of a simpler time. The enduring issues—those that have concerned us over the last seventy-five years and are likely to remain with us—fall into two categories: those affecting evaluation in the classroom and those applying to tests from beyond the classroom.

Teacher-made Tests

Teacher-made tests dominate the daily experience of students. Snap quizzes, pop quizzes, unit tests, weekly tests, oral tests, chapter tests, quarterlies, midterms, finals, makeups, term papers, research papers, five-paragraph essays, eleven-paragraph essays—in myriad ways, teachers test, retest, and test again. How good are the tests?

John Goodlad, whose research teams observed thousands of hours of instruction for the Study of Schooling, writes:

> Remember the Friday morning spelling test? It's still there. Most of the elementary teachers in our sample listed it. . . . Standardized tests often were used at both junior and senior high levels for placing students in classes. Teacher-made tests at these levels appeared to be designed and used, not for diagnosis, but for assessing and marking students' achievement as well as for controlling students' behavior. At all levels, these tests called almost exclusively for short answers and recall of information. Workbooks and worksheets, often a part of daily instruction, were used cumulatively by many teachers to mark pupil

> progress and achievement. These frequently were duplicated from commercial materials. The directions given on worksheets often were "copy the sentence" or "circle each verb" or "combine two sentences into one" or "add correct punctuation." If teachers gave tests involving writing paragraphs or essays, they seldom so indicated.[1]

Studies done by Arthur Applebee[2] and results of several national writing assessments[3] indicate that surprisingly few English teachers provide feedback to their students on their essays. National Assessment of Educational Progress results showed, for instance, that only one teacher of seventeen-year-olds in five both provides suggestions on papers and discusses them with students. Of those teachers who do provide feedback, most only comment upon spelling, mechanics, grammar, and usage, and require little rewriting.

The short-answer, fill-in-the-blank, and recall tests that predominate in the classroom reinforce three aspects of current pedagogy that keep it inefficient and vulnerable to constant criticism. They place a premium on rote learning and memorization, driving out time for problem solving or applying knowledge. They contribute to the fragmentation of knowledge that has already progressed so far that few students can rise above it. And they deprive students of opportunities to think hard about anything, or to apply such higher-order thinking skills as interpretation or evaluation.

Consequently, teacher-made tests represent an enduring evaluation issue. As long as many teachers continue to test and grade as the above studies indicate they do, there will be calls for more "objective" or trustworthy kinds of evaluation. As long as teacher-made tests stress short answers and recall of "facts," commercial standardized tests will most likely do the same, reinforcing teachers in that practice. As long as English teachers focus almost entirely upon grammar, usage, mechanics, spelling, and knowledge of literary facts and terms, active learning will take a back seat to passive test-taking. Learning and evaluation will not be working in tandem.

Tests from Outside the Classroom

It is useful to make a distinction between tests designed to serve direct educational purposes and tests that function primarily as management tools. In the first category I would put any test that helps a teacher and a student concretely understand what the student is learning or failing to learn; provides students with opportunities to demonstrate knowledge and skills in appropriate contexts; is itself a learning experience for both student and teacher; and helps students to develop and even practice evaluative systems of their own. In the second I would put any test that serves primarily to rank students for management decisions (e.g., admissions, program assignment, school or district comparisons); provides primarily quantitative and relational, not substantive, information to student, teacher, and others; and is not directly tied to what the student has been studying in the classroom, since it was created apart from and prior to the student's course of study.

Most tests from beyond the classroom fall into the second category. Although they are often rationalized as educational instruments, they create information far more relevant to management decisions than to learning or instruction. The critique of these commercial, norm-referenced, standardized tests is lengthy. The research upon which they rest is not compelling; they employ formats and text seen nowhere else in students' lives; they are often culturally biased; they focus too heavily upon recollection of facts and draw primarily upon lower-level cognitive skills; they do not offer serious learning opportunities; and they are too often misused and misrepresented.[4]

As management tools, only obliquely related to learning, the tests don't have to be perfectly accurate or comprehensive. They just have to be rough estimators. No one needs to "prove" that inferences drawn from them are definitive; a plausible case will suffice. An analogy might be the Dow-Jones average, which badly misrepresents the situation of specific stocks, portfolios, or companies, and, like numerous economic indicators, is crude and open to flagrant misuse and contradictory interpretations—yet it and the others constitute the meat and drink of policy discourse. It is simply a reality of our times that social and economic indicators appear necessary, are always too abstract, and are technically problematic and controversial.

Norm-referenced tests are sorting devices that enable us to arrange large numbers of data points on a scale; that is all they do. When schools or districts use commercial tests, they are "evaluating" only in the sense that they are ranking individuals and schools and tracking changes in these rankings. Little can be determined about what the students know or how well the teachers teach; all one can know from these tests is that some students score higher than others or some schools' average scores are higher than others'.

Granting that this is very limited information, one can nevertheless use it to question the instruction a particular child receives. You can put aside entirely the fact that a test may be measuring the wrong things in the wrong way if the test results cause the right people to ask why the Anglo children are getting higher scores than the Hispanics or why rich schools have higher scores than poor schools or why reading scores are going up but math scores are going down. Questions such as these have sparked important dialogues, and have led to concrete actions, legal and otherwise, aimed at improving educational opportunities for all children. So while it may be true that commercial, standardized, norm-referenced tests do not substantially help the English teacher teach and evaluate, they may, under the best circumstances, make significant long-term contributions both to education and to social justice.

The enduring issues with respect to tests from beyond the classroom cluster around specific tests or around the concept of mass testing itself. For specific tests, the issues are:

1. Whether or not the test is closely related to what students have been taught
2. Whether the ways a test measures knowledges and skills are valid (in the common-sense meaning of that word)
3. Whether the test is fair to all who take it
4. Whether the results of the test constitute sufficient or appropriate grounds for the educational management decisions one wishes to make

For mass testing, the issues are these:

1. Is too much class time being consumed by tests that relate only marginally to learning and instruction?
2. Are test results being used properly by school officials, administrators, school boards, the press, and policy makers?
3. Does mass testing unfairly stigmatize or penalize certain population groups? Does it increase or foreclose opportunity?
4. Does large-scale testing affect the curriculum (a) at all? and, if so, (b) beneficially? or (c) negatively?

Over the last fifteen years, English teachers have vigorously discussed these issues at NCTE meetings and at school, district, and state meetings of various kinds. Many teachers have helped develop assessments that meet, and in some cases actually raise, professional standards. Where there is suspicion that a test is invalid or unfair, or is being misused, the test can be taken to court. All in all, it appears the profession is making slow, steady progress in defining its standards with respect to specific tests of reading, writing, literature, speaking, and listening.

Progress with respect to mass testing is more difficult to gauge. Is too much classroom time spent on profitless testing? Each school must answer that question for itself. Are test results used properly? There is evidence that in many places they are not. SAT scores should not be used as indicators of school quality, but the entire nation has assumed otherwise.

Schools should not be ranked solely in terms of standardized test scores, but the practice is commonplace. The press and others will use such indicators until we give them better ones.

Does mass testing unfairly stigmatize groups whose performance is "below average"? Yes. But I wonder whether those groups would receive the extra attention and resources they need if there were no test results upon which to base arguments for more attention and resources. Has mass testing brought about greater opportunity for minorities or has it shunted minorities onto tracks leading to second-class educations and jobs? Paul Ramsey addresses these questions in the essay that follows.

Does mass testing affect the curriculum? It is tempting to say that *nothing* affects the curriculum—yet it's sensible to believe that minimum competency tests may narrow what is taught. If that is so, it is equally sensible to believe that more imaginative and comprehensive evaluations—whether teacher-made or commercial—might broaden or deepen the curriculum or change the ways we teach English over the next seventy-five years.

Minorities and Standardized Tests

P. A. Ramsey

As for the issue of whether mass tests are fair to all who take them, when minorities and testing are discussed, what is almost always being talked about is the fact that a number of students, most of whom are black, Hispanic, or Native American, and many of whom are from the lower part of the socioeconomic scale, do more poorly on standardized multiple-choice tests than do middle- and upper-class students, most of whom are white. "Minority" then is used in our country's doublespeak as a designate of race as well as of socioeconomic standing, while "testing" denotes standardized, most often multiple-choice, examinations.

The two terms, minority and testing, are seldom brought together without producing electricity. The electricity comes when concerned educators look at the standardized test scores of minority students vis-à-vis the scores of majority students. The minority group scores are invariably lower. If they weren't, there would be something wrong—a broken computer spewing out erroneous scores or an unreliable test inadvertently constructed and administered. If the average white student did as poorly on standardized tests as does the average black, Hispanic, or Native American, we would know that God was not in His/Her heaven and all was not right with the world. But the world is right, not turned upside down; minority students do more poorly on these tests.

When concerned people see this status quo, i.e., minority students doing more poorly yet again, the electricity mentioned above turns on, as it were, the fan, and what is blown about is the word "bias" by at least three distinct minority voices.

The Voices

One voice, perhaps the most strident, uses bias in testing to mean racist policy or intent in testing. To the person who equates test bias with racism, a biased test or question is one that discriminates against minority students. In such an equation there is always the undercurrent—perhaps undertow—of volition: "You made this test like this to hurt our children." Yet intent really does not matter when you look at the results of standardized testing. Whether the tests are willfully designed to hurt minority students is in many ways a purely academic matter if, indeed, they do hurt these students by denying them access to the best classes, schools, jobs, or whatever.

At another place on the spectrum of minority responses are those who say that the problem is not so much with the tests as with the educational system. Kenneth Clark has said that being upset with tests because minority students do poorly on them is like being upset with a thermometer because it tells you that you have a fever. For proponents of this position it is not the tests but the educational system that is biased. What differential performance on tests reflects is different educational opportunities. The idea of a racist educational system is interesting to consider in a discussion of testing because some research suggests that some standardized tests overpredict for minority students, i.e., their scores on the tests—even though low—indicate that they should get better grades in school than they do. One possible interpretation for these lower grades is that the tests may be biased but not as biased as our classrooms.

A third minority response to the testing problem is in some ways the most recent response in that it moves beyond (perhaps behind, depending on your perspective) the bias debates that grew out of the so-called liberal concerns of the 1960s. It argues that the reason minority students do poorly on standardized tests—bias willful or unwillful, racist test or racist educational system—is irrelevant. Minority students must pass the tests, and the job of educators is to teach them to do so.

Which of the three minority responses above is right? Of course, to some degree they all are: Of course, to some extent the tests or at least some of the questions on them are biased in that they favor some groups over others. Of course, the educational system in this country is racist. The economically lower classes, which are filled with minority people, do not, as a rule, receive as good an education as do those in the middle and upper classes. Boards of education care no more about the poor than does the rest of society, and racists are found in front of the classroom, just as they are found in the marketplace and in the church.

Possible Responses

Minority students must be taught to pass the tests, but how? It is the answer to this "how" that is so frustrating because we know so little about test bias, its causes and how to remedy it. Sure evidence of racism is neither in our tests nor in our classrooms but in our ignorance. Indeed, the labyrinth of test bias is still too complex for the simple instruments of analysis we have developed thus far. Yet this much is known: We would without a doubt know more about bias in tests if white students over the last generation had done as poorly as minority students have on standardized tests! We'd either know more or there would be different tests.

Soon we will know more. Major testing programs, such as the SAT, are now very concerned about bias and are therefore studying it. Educators must keep the pressure on all testing companies to see that they are constantly furthering our understanding of test bias—what causes it and what can be done to minimize it.

In a practical vein, what can teachers do? First and foremost, make sure that, before your school system adopts a standardized test, there is information about differential racial and sexual performance on that test. If test suppliers cannot supply this information, find another test, but if you do decide not to adopt a test because of the paucity or nonexistence of such information—a lack that will undoubtedly be explained in monetary terms: "Such studies cost so much"—make sure the testing company knows why you or your system decided not to use its test.

Second, whenever possible, teachers should take the standardized tests their students are to take, not for the purpose of sharing with their students specific answers to questions, but so as to better interpret for their students the doublespeak of test directions and test questions and to share the test-taking strategies gained only by actually taking tests. Much is to be learned from the test-taking experience, an experience most professional adults have gladly repressed.

As teachers, we must make sure that students do not go into the test-taking situation "cold." Before they open their test books, students should know the format of the questions they will be encountering and understand the directions. Students need to be initiated into the idiolect or doublespeak of multiple-choice testing and the particular way that idiolect will be manifested in the tests they are to take. Undoubtedly, one of the main reasons many minority students do not do as well as white students on standardized tests is that minority students are not as well prepared to take tests as are their white counterparts.

Many point out that familiarization courses—at least those outside of the school curriculum—are too expensive for many minority students. That may well be the case, but such courses are not the only way for students to become familiar with particular standardized tests. For a nominal fee, students can obtain retired and practice tests from most of the major testing companies. Students should procure their test-preparation materials, when possible, from the company that makes the test they plan to take, since this company, more than any other test-preparation company, will have practice materials with questions most like those that will be scored. In some programs, an analysis of the zip codes of those students requesting disclosed tests has shown that it is generally students from upper-middle-class neighborhoods who are availing themselves of these most inexpensive test preparation materials. It is not surprising that students from more affluent families are availing themselves—part of being advantaged is knowing what to avail yourself of—but it is discouraging that teachers and counselors within the minority communities are apparently not also encouraging their students to avail themselves of these resources, or if they are encouraging their students, their plea seems to be unheeded. One mandatory sophomore or junior English class writing assignment asking every student to compose a letter to a testing company requesting study materials for a particular test, in every high school in the country which has a sizeable minority population, would do much toward at least putting the proper test-preparation materials into minority students' hands. Indeed, such an assignment would almost surely do more for most students than would a five-page essay on a topic of their or anyone else's choice.

Ironically, teachers often do quite a bit to make the task of test-taking more difficult for minority students. Unwittingly, minority teachers may be the most culpable in this one area. Quite often minority students are programmed for failure, psyched-out long before they open that test book, by what their teachers have communicated to them both verbally and nonverbally about standardized tests. Psychologically it is quite a different matter to go into an already tense test-taking situation believing that if you are prepared you at least have the opportunity to succeed than it is to go into that tense situation believing that the test is designed to make you fail and, therefore, that there is really nothing you can do to help yourself. Educators do minority students no favor when they inflict their own biases about testing onto them, playing into their students' fears, and thereby making an already difficult situation—test-taking—nigh impossible.

The most important thing that teachers can do to help minority test-takers is to teach them the requisite skills to succeed, in particular the skills of reading, writing, and analysis. Most multiple-choice tests are ultimately reading tests. If your students are poor readers, they are almost surely going to have problems with a timed, paper-and-pencil, multiple-choice test. Poor readers simply must be identified and given every possible opportunity to learn to read.

Testing Writing

Of special concern to English teachers are multiple-choice and essay tests of writing ability. We do not like testing writing with multiple-choice questions; most of us don't even think it can be done.

A major criticism of multiple-choice writing tests is that the questions are little more than prescriptive grammatical error hunting. Certain types of questions, e.g., the type which asks students to identify the underlined error, are little more than that. Of course, in teaching that important facet of the composing process, editing skills, you are training the eye and ear to hunt for errors. Even so, the more sophisticated multiple-choice questions which force students to assess style and manipulate language are probably deserving of more credit than the profession gives them. They really test an ability or skill which is essential to effective writing—a student's sense of language, his/her grammatical intuition: "Does it sound/read right?" This skill is at the heart of the revising process.

Without a doubt, the best writing test has both a multiple-choice and an essay component. Together these sections increase both reliability (the extent to which the scores of a group of students will remain consistent if these students take a test again and have neither learned nor forgotten the subject matter since the previous testing time) and validity (the assurance that a test is assessing what we hope to assess, e.g., the ability to write rather than the ability to find errors). Between a multiple-choice and an essay writing test, most of us would choose to assess writing ability through the essay because of its high validity, that is, that it tests what we really want to know: Can a student generate, organize, and develop rhetorically effective prose? The presence of essays on national standardized writing tests is also a prod to the less industrious of the profession to give their students writing assignments rather than just worksheets.

In all fairness, though, it must be acknowledged that essay testing has its own set of problems. One of them is that the typical essay-testing situation is so stilted: Usually, writing is being assessed and a score given on the basis of a one-shot, timed, first-draft writing sample. This is better than no writing sample at all, but the writing situation is decidedly limited and artificial. Multiple writing assignments given at different times that ask for writing in different modes and with different aims would constitute the best essay-testing situation, but for national standardized tests the money and time factors make such ideal testing impossible.

There is also the difficulty of setting uniform standards for readers. Ironically, the matter of test bias is usually not mentioned when essay testing is discussed. It should be, for there is much we need to know and be careful about in this area. For example, does one type of scoring—holistic, analytic, primary-trait—seem to favor or disfavor minority students more than does another type? Do essay writing tests better assess the writing ability of minority students than do multiple-choice writing tests? When multiple-choice writing questions are used, do certain types prove to be easier or more difficult for minority students than they do for majority ones? It is the lack of information on these issues more than the tests or the teaching which suggests the racism of malign neglect.

As a former English teacher and present employee of one of the largest testing agencies, I believe that it is the collective power of educators that will change the world of testing for the better. If you do not believe that you can change the monolithic world of testing, just remember that when the essay was taken out of the ATP English Composition Test, it was the English teachers of this country who insisted that it be put back in, and it was. When you, the people who use the tests, unite and speak, your voice is heard and, to paraphrase Sir Philip Sidney, it moves—though it may not delight—the makers of standardized tests.

Notes

1. J. Goodlad, *A Place Called School: Prospects for the Future* (New York: McGraw-Hill, 1984), 207.
2. Arthur Applebee, *Writing in the Secondary School* (Urbana, Ill.: National Council of Teachers of English, 1981).
3. R. Brown and the National Assessment of Educational Progress Staff, *Writing Achievement, 1969–79,* 3 vols. (Denver: Education Commission of the States, 1980–81).

4. Charles W. Daves, ed., *The Uses and Misuses of Tests* (San Francisco: Jossey-Bass, 1984); Stephen J. Gould, *The Mismeasure of Man* (New York: Norton, 1981); Banesh Hoffman, *The Tyranny of Testing* (New York: Crowell Collier, 1962); Paul L. Houts, ed., *The Myth of Measurability* (New York: Hart, 1977); Martin Nystrand, "The Politics of Rank Ordering," *English Journal* 64 (Mar. 1975): 42–45; and Andrew J. Strenio, Jr., *The Testing Trap: How It Can Make or Break Your Career and Your Children's Futures* (New York: Rawson, Wade, 1981).

9 Books and the New Technologies

Charles Suhor

For the second time in less than two decades, the question is being raised: Are textbooks—indeed, books in general—becoming obsolete? The question was considered revolutionary during the media movement of the late 1960s and early 1970s, when Marshall McLuhan and others called into doubt the permanency of print culture in Western civilization. Since English and language arts teachers have traditionally been the custodians of two of the three R's, the response within the National Council of Teachers of English was particularly energetic.

Articles appeared in *English Journal* and *Elementary English* with titles like "Hook Up, Plug In, Connect: Relevancy Is All" and "The Times They Are A'Changing?" [1] According to John Dixon participants at the 1966 Dartmouth Seminar "accepted the view that 'literature' includes a television presentation as well as the printed book, and that both are the responsibility of the English Department. The making of a tape or film . . . may become as natural forms of presentation as the making of a magazine."[2]

Some of the bolder predictions made during the late sixties are echoed by recent predictions about the decline of books. In 1969, for example, Malcolm Griffith and Earl Seidman wrote, "Our guess is that eventually books may well disappear—just as the wandering bards gradually disappeared after the invention of print. . . . In the future, information will be moved electronically (the computer will replace the library)."[3] A 1981 report by Sally Zakariya includes similar predictions. "Reading may lose its place as the primary criterion of academic success, with computer literacy overtaking it as education's number one priority. . . . Within five years, the laser videodisk will take its place beside the microcomputer in the nation's homes and classrooms."[4] In the same year, Frederick Praeger, president of Westview Press, flatly stated, "The world of author and publisher as we know it is dead."[5]

Given the undependability of futurists' pronouncements, it is no wonder that teachers have been, in Ronald Hunt's words, "reluctant to jump" when new hoops of technology are brought into the ring. Hunt points out that teachers were told to "get with it" when language laboratories, educational television, and other new media were introduced, yet those technologies did not take firm hold in the schools.[6] Clearly, major technological changes in society do not necessarily result in wholesale curricular changes in schools. The invention of the automobile changed our way of living but did not result in school programs dominated by engine tuneups, car careers, or automobile literacy.

I am not arguing that we should be complacent about the relationship between books and the new technologies in English language arts instruction. We don't really *know* whether the school uses of emerging technologies are mere fads or early signs of a radically changed curriculum, or something in between. My goal in this chapter is not to debunk but to offer some perspectives, based on a historical overview and on recent research and theory concerning the relations between books and nonprint media in English. Against this background, I'll discuss the current tensions between books and electronic technologies in English language arts instruction. Finally, in dealing with the future I won't indulge in breathless prognostication but will make some conservative projections (i.e., guesses) with the frank admission that I am in the business of making self-fulfilling prophecies.

The Historical Background

It is important to see the relationship of books and other means of communication—from the spoken word to the nonverbal arts to satellite transmission—in a historical perspective. The literacy chart on pages 98–99 is an attempt to outline ways in which preliterate cultures differ in fundamental ways from literate cultures, and to show how our emerging multiliterate culture is related to preliterate and literate cultures.

I admit at the outset that such charts are risky business; they require that complex social and psychological phenomena be presented in scandalous shorthand. They cannot reveal important historical and cross-cultural refinements. For example, although the Greek phonetic alphabet was invented around 900 B.C. and the printing press around A.D. 1450, mass literacy was not even thinkable until the mid- to late nineteenth century, when inventions like the steam-powered cylindrical press made mass production possible.[7] And the study of contemporary nonliterate cultures shows that "literacy" is not synonymous with ability to do highly abstract thinking and systematic reasoning.[8]

However, some important points about the historical context of literacy are illustrated in the chart, the most obvious being that the present revolution in electronic media is part of a long and complex evolution in human communication. Moreover, the clusters of characteristics associated with preliterate/literate/multiliterate cultures provide an interesting backdrop for reflections on education. The suppression of critical functions in preliterate and multiliterate cultures is of particular interest, as is the fact that the multiliterate culture in many ways resembles preliterate cultures more than literate ones.[9]

Having pointed to some of the rich contexts for the discussion of textbooks and technologies, we must go on to define some of the problems in terms of education in our own time. I'll explore the media movement of the late sixties and early seventies and then examine the current state of our understanding of electronic technologies in the English language arts curriculum.

The First Electronic Revolution: What Happened?

The McLuhan revolution, as Ronald Hunt suggests, did not quite materialize on schedule. This was disappointing to the English teachers who were at the forefront of the movement, teaching elective courses in areas such as mass media, television study, film study, and filmmaking. I was among a group of English educators (e.g., Bruce Appleby, John Culkin, Art Daigon, Charles Grenier, Patrick Hazard, Herb Karl, Fred Marcus, Charles Weinburger) who frequently contributed to *Media & Methods,* the pace-setting journal of the time. It seemed to us that the English teaching profession, true to the Dartmouth statement, was headed toward a multimedia curriculum, with viewing of films taking a place beside the reading of books and videotaping of student drama beside the writing of short stories. Yet by the mid-seventies the back to basics advocates were successfully attacking the study and use of nonprint media as "frills" in both the popular press and in educational circles.

The decline of support for media in English was surprisingly swift and effective, and a look at the reasons for that decline sheds light on the present interest in new technologies. In 1981 I did a study of the nature and extent of the English teaching profession's involvement in the media movement, exploring questions like these: Was the movement undergirded by clear rationales, or was the flurry of media activity in English classes by and large a tinkertoy effort? I examined the literature of English education and related fields, 1961 through 1978, with particular attention to four NCTE journals—*English Journal, Elementary English/Language Arts, College English,* and *College Composition and Communication.*

The 1961–78 period spans the years of McLuhan's major influence and moves into the back-to-basics movement; therefore, the quantitative and qualitative patterns found in published materials during that time were

LITERACY CHART

	Preliterate Cultures	*Literate Cultures*	*Multiliterate Cultures*
World Views	Totalistic, magical, organic, communal; history as inherited wisdom.	Hierarchical, fragmented, individualistic; rationally based; history as progressive.	Unifying, holographic, cosmic (e.g., relationships among sciences/Eastern philosophy); history as teleological.
Arts	Multisensory, integrated, mythopoeic, rooted in ritual; simple formulary devices; artists/consumers part of community.	Differentiated, specialized; tending to discursiveness, analysis; genre distinctions; highly wrought forms; individual artist as hero; elite consumers.	Multisensory, multigenre forms, channels, and peformances (mobile sculptures, concrete poetry, aleatory music, television, participatory drama); mythic themes, prototypes; mass participatory consumers.
Language	Fluid, context-bound; nonstandard, serving aesthetic and communal goals.	Rule-based, logical; less context-dependent, more propositional; standardization meets commercial, social, scientific needs.	Semiotic perspective—language important as one of many mutually supportive sign systems in the making of meaning.
Education	Home- and village-centered; oral tradition; maxims, tales, epigrammatic wisdom dominate; knowledge seen as static; simple indoctrination.	Bureaucratically organized schools; separate subject areas, segmented classrooms, timetables, deadlines; knowledge as serial, incremental; complex indoctrination.	Partially at home via electronic technologies; child-centered instruction, lifelong learning; cooperative learning, education for "learning to learn"—low indoctrination; knowledge as perceiving interrelationships.

Social Memory	Resides with people—folk art, oral tradition, oral history.	Resides in texts and with elite—scribes, priests, scholars.	Resides in complex information-storage systems—access through mass education; TV as basis for popular social memory.
Social Attitudes	Cohesion, accommodation; tribal loyalty, low critique of orally transmitted tradition; elders revered as repositories of values.	Individualism, competition, ambition, acquisitiveness; high critique of tradition (via printed records); elders passé.	Empathy, identification, cooperation, perspective-taking; low critique of tradition (due to information overload, primacy of moving images), elders regarded ambivalently because of health, wealth, power, numbers.
Work	Part of tribal involvement, larger web of human relationships; worker, nature, tools and product closely interrelated.	Isolated tasks for pay; division of labor; assembly lines, bureaucracies, protocols; workers remote from raw materials, mechanical tools, products.	Revival of communal work atmosphere via medieval/oriental models; emphasis on social responsibility; corporate images in ads; work at home via computer-driven technologies.

quite revealing.[10] In the four journals studied intensively, media-related articles increased consistently over the eighteen-year period (with some suggestion of a decline in the final two years under study).

But a close look at the *kinds* of articles in the journals revealed a slim theoretical base for the media movement. There was no shortage of practical articles (334 in all) enthusiastically describing classroom activities that involve the new media; but few such articles were accompanied by well-developed rationales or strong statements of theoretical bases for use of media in English. Moreover, there were only 83 analytical articles—i.e., in-depth analyses of nonprint media works—and about half of those relied wholly on literary terms and approaches to analysis, to the exclusion of the tools of analysis peculiar to the medium under study. One hundred fifty-eight articles dealt with equipment and machinery—a respectable showing at first glance, yet by far the most frequently discussed piece of equipment was the tape recorder, followed by the computer. Unlike more recent (and far more abundant) articles on computers in English, earlier articles tended to be caveat pieces expressing reservations about what computers can and should do in the classroom.

Two bright spots appeared in the eighteen-year review of media and English. First, there were the materials I called "qualitative"—i.e., 144 articles dealing with broadly qualitative aspects of media, such as the effects of television on students' reading habits and the use of electronic media as instruments of propaganda. These articles frequently yielded considerable insight into the social and cognitive effects of media. Of greater interest were the theoretical articles. A total of 390 articles offered *some* kind of rationale for media in English. However, only 90 theoretical statements went beyond brief, undeveloped comments. Articles firmly based in theory were quite exceptional. Most noteworthy were Patrick Hazard's early (1956–63) *English Journal* columns on media and Nancy Cromer Thompson's later series (1975–78), both of which included sustained, lucid arguments for using and studying media in English programs.

Overall, the strongest rationales for media in English—mainly found in articles written during the last years included in the study—were based on semiotics, aesthetic education, and learning theory.[11] Some keen theoretical analyses were found in sources outside of the NCTE journals.[12] But again, such rationales were rare; it is fair to say that the media movement of the late 1960s and early 1970s was to a large extent a gaggle of gimmicks. The very weakness of the movement paved the way for the basics backlash that followed.

Experimental research and status studies during the media movement were, on the whole, not enlightening. Educational technology specialists conducted innumerable experiments comparing the effectiveness of different media in teaching various kinds of materials—in English and in other disciplines as well. Commentators on experimental research in *Educational Communication and Technology* (formerly *AV Communication Review*) consistently pointed to inconclusive results and lack of a unifying conceptual framework for media-related research.

Status studies of English teachers' actual use of and attitudes toward media suggested that classroom teachers were far less enthusiastic about media than were writers for professional journals.[13] Kenneth Donelson, for example, surveyed 201 Arizona English teachers judged highly capable by their department heads. The teachers made little use of media, even though equipment and materials were available. R. V. Barry surveyed 150 schools that had been included in the 1968 Squire and Applebee study of outstanding English programs.[14] He found that educational media—as a pedagogical method, as an academic subject, or as part of a student-oriented learning process—were not strongly supported by English department heads or teachers. Even though the *English Journal* (viewed by Barry, quite justifiably, as basically a pro-media publication) was the teachers' main source of information, they preferred basic skills approaches to instruction. They saw media as nonessential and used media hardware infrequently, even as audiovisual aids. Similarly, A. J. Roberts found that media were used infrequently, even among English teachers who believed media to be important. Moreover, most teachers did not see mass media as an appropriate topic for serious study.

Such was the sad fate of the media movement of the late 1960s and early 1970s, viewed with the benefit of hindsight—and with a fair amount of research and testimony. If we look at data available for the current technology movement, some useful insights emerge.

The New Electronic Era: What's Happening?

In terms of experimental research bases for the new technologies in the classroom, educational technologists still find little cause to celebrate. Richard E. Clark reviewed comparison studies from the 1960s through 1983, including recent metanalyses of CAI (computer-assisted instruction), and concluded that "we will not find learning differences that can be unambiguously attributed to any medium of instruction."[15]

Clark noted, though, that recent research has explored some new dimensions of media. Researchers in the 1970s saw promise in semiotics-based notions like "media attributes"[16]—the qualities through which certain media induce models of particular cognitive skills in learners. For example, students can learn to attend to significant cues by seeing films in which the camera "zooms in" on pertinent details. The choice of symbol system (i.e., iconic) and of mechanical technology and delivery (i.e., film and zooming) resulted in improved cue-attending that would not occur, for example, in reading about how to sharpen one's observational skills.

Such research is a far cry from easily confounded comparison studies in which group A learns a concept from a computer program while group B learns it from a teacher's presentation. But even attribute research proved disappointing. For example, in followups to the "zooming" experiment, different mechanical devices or techniques of delivery proved as effective as "zooming in." The isolation of relevant cues, not the choice of medium or symbol system, was the pertinent variable. Perhaps Clark's conclusions about the continued impoverishment of theory-based media research and his negative views about comparison research are excessive.[17] But few would deny that the state of the art of experimental research in instructional technology is inconclusive at best.

What of research on new technologies related more specifically to English and language arts? One would have to be happy with a less than half-filled cup to be excited about recent research, most of it focused on computers. Status studies from the Center for Social Organization of Schools showed students using computers in isolation (rather than in groups) more frequently in English study than in math, science, or social studies.[18] The center also found that during English study, students awaiting their turns at the computer most frequently did seatwork (rather than small-group or whole-class work, which were more common as "waiting time" activities in other subjects). A 1983 National Education Association report showed that only 5.3 percent of the elementary and secondary teachers surveyed used computers to teach writing, as compared to use by 16 percent in teaching grammar, 34.7 percent in teaching reading, and 70.7 percent in teaching mathematics.[19]

There are problems, too, with computer-assisted instruction programs. Complaints about low-quality software are legion. Research reports on CAI are not persuasive, as in the positive effects of CAI reported by Educational Testing Service in Los Angeles city schools, where the software students used was solely drill and practice material. On the optimistic side, both the NEA and the Educational Products Information Exchange report recent improvement in software, the latter citing a 90 percent increase in 1984 in logic and problem-solving programs.[20] Moreover, W. Patrick Dickson points to the development of "thought-provoking software," in which "the computer's capacity to provide rapid translation between symbol systems (e.g., oral, verbal, pictorial)" is used.[21]

Dickson's semiotic perspective is especially interesting because it suggests that high-quality software has the potential to present multimedia learning experiences that cannot be provided in books. Of the ten kinds of software programs he describes, six make strong use of verbal abilities in mind-stretching exercises that work across symbol systems, and several inherently involve social interaction. Among the programs cited by Dickson is John Henry Martin's "Writing to Read" system, which uses computers, audiocassettes, typewriters, student journals, and other media.

The question of whether the computer normally promotes or frustrates student interaction is not easily answered. Dickson cites research evidence indicating that, at the least, it cannot be said that computers in the classroom typically hamper interaction. (He might have added that there is nothing in books that makes them inherently conducive to interaction.) Colette Daiute's more intensive analysis of the socializing effects of computers in the teaching of writing, though, concludes that numerous factors are more important than the computer in stimulating interaction in programs that make use of word processors. She cites changes in the teacher's writing philosophy, the teacher's approach to using computers, students' work styles, and "accidents" (e.g., shared learning because of a limited number of computers) as important and largely unexamined aspects of the relation between computer use and student interaction.[22]

Nevertheless, it is clear that the most significant potential for computers in the English program has been demonstrated in word processing. And surely the integration of writing process instruction with word processing would involve less dependence on textbooks (although texts modeled explicitly on process instruction are increasing). Moreover, dependence on handbooks, memorization of rules of grammar and spelling, and even CAI drill software would be greatly reduced with the availability of text editing systems that include spelling checks, highlighting of trite phrases and grammatical errors, etc.

Indeed, if word processing becomes a normal mode of teaching composition, we will see a controversy over text editors in the English language arts similar to that in mathematics over the use of hand calculators. Do students need to know mathematical "tables" when a calculator is always at hand? Do they need to know rules of spelling and punctuation when the text editor will signal many of the problems? Another practical question is that of keyboard skills. Despite frequent anecdotes about how easily young children take to keyboards, Diane Rothenberg's review of research shows that children's greatest frustration in using computers springs from problems in keystroking.[23] Keyboard skills might be less of a problem at higher levels, where students frequently have studied typing or have stronger motivation to learn rapid keystroking.

The most exciting and innovative contributions of the word processor are in the area of revision, since writers no longer need to rewrite entire texts when making changes. But 1977 National Assessment of Educational

Progress research on student revision suggests that few students actually know how to make significant revisions, even when given the opportunity;[24] and, as Daiute suggests, teachers must understand and implement writing process instruction in order to take advantage of the computer as a tool for revision. Massive inservice training will be required in process-based composition instruction and in the mechanics of word processing, and few models for such inservice exist.[25] An encouraging, if ironic, prospect is that the current interest in the word processor as a compositional tool will give further impetus to sound preservice and inservice instruction in how to teach writing.

Even skeptics must acknowledge that English and language arts researchers are learning much about how word processors can be used in teaching composition, from invention through proofreading.[26] And regarding CAI, the message is out that simple-minded software will not do. Various consumer groups and teacher organizations are helping to set the direction of software development and evaluation.[27]

How might other new technologies—interactive video and voice-activated typewriters, for instance—affect the role of books in English instruction? Interactive video has been described by Samuel Howe as a technology "that combines the best audiovisual features of video with the calculation, power, and speed of the computer."[28] In the sciences, the claim is already being made that videodiscs can show things that are "virtually impossible to present in textbooks."[29] Howe says that interactive video "may replace the computer, the instructional film, educational video, and perhaps even textbooks."

Many participants in a University of Connecticut Delphi study of the impact of technology on the future of English teaching cited interactive fiction via videodisc as a sign of the future.[30] There are technical and financial limitations, though, on the development of interactive video materials. Videodisc players are relatively inexpensive ($400 to $700), but linking them with microcomputers and programming good instructional components is a technical skill well beyond the ken of most teachers. Commercially developed videodiscs are scarce, and the lack of a ready school market has discouraged an investment in sophisticated educational videodiscs. Rockley Miller, editor of *Videodisc Monitor,* calls it "a chicken and egg problem." Industry sees a meager market, and "you can't sell schools [videodisc players] on the promise that software will be available eventually."[31]

The voice-recognition dictation system, or voice-activated typewriter (VAT), is waiting in the wings of both industry and education. VAT goes from voice directly to screen. It is connected to a personal computer and involves minimal keyboard skills. Consequently, a major hurdle is removed: the composer need not learn a novel psychomotor skill—viz., the ability to type rapidly enough to keep up with the flow of ideas. All the advantages of the word processor are there, but the whole question of teaching keyboard skills becomes moot.

Of course, VAT poses some new problems. Hardware costs are still astronomical, by school standards. Moreover, the art of dictation is a form of composing that differs in important ways from writing by hand, typing, or using a word processor. Routine or brief materials are easily formulated in dictation, but dictation of long and complex material minimally requires sketchy notes and some unique development of aural imagery. The aural dependency is diminished greatly in VAT, however, since the screen shows the words as they are dictated, and many find composing-by-dictation to be an accessible skill.

Current VAT technology, however, adds burdens beyond mere skill in formal oral composing. Most machines require that each word be pronounced separately, without elision, and only after the computer has "learned" certain features of the individual composer's dialect. Several manufacturers produce VATs, but the largest vocabulary now available is 10,000 words. We can expect advancements, however, in VAT technology, and prices will surely come down. Both MIT and Carnegie-Mellon University, for instance, have grants to develop better "talk-writers."[32] So the complex relations between speaking and writing will take on even more subtle dimensions in the future, and if VAT reaches the classroom the teaching of composition will become even less bound by the conventions of textbooks.

The Future—Again

In describing the current technology movement, I've been unable to avoid some discussion of the future. We are obviously in a state of change; a bit of speculation about next steps is inevitable. Understandably, we wonder how teachers can teach revision with word processors unless we undertake ambitious teacher-training programs. We can't help asking whether the voice-activated typewriter will ultimately solve problems of teaching keyboarding. It is as human to speculate as it is to err.

It is useful to remember, though, that most prognostications, in the social sciences at least, have simply proved to be errors made in advance. Hence, it is foolish to burden our guesses with the weight of prophecy and to puff them in statements like "It isn't too blue-sky to say that by 2000, personal computers will also be desk-top video conference sites"—a sentence from a 1985 news article ironically entitled "Video Conference Slow to Catch On."[33]

The Biblical definition of a prophet is someone who has a message for humankind from God. For most of us, then, predictions aren't prophecies but expressions either of wishful thinking or dread, and as such they should be spurs to action. When I "predict" that the portable, foldable, tactilely unique paperback will never lose its utility, I am expressing fond hopes and perhaps laying the basis for programmatic action. I believe that the only prophecies worth making (by mere mortals, at least) are those that are self-fulfilling by reason of our determination to make them come true. Consequently, I take very seriously the prediction about reading being replaced by computer literacy, because I suspect that people who make that kind of prediction will be working like hell to see that it comes to pass. I like my predictions about the future of technologies and books much better, and if I don't try to fulfill them, I'll not only be in error but at fault. Viewed from this perspective, Delphi surveys are advanced parlor games, and prediction without activism is flapdoodle.

Having warned you of that, I'll go ahead and predict the future of books and other technologies in the English classroom. In the short run, books will continue to get a great deal of attention, and they might even get better because of the current concern about the "dumbing down" of textbooks and the recently resurrected worry about the bowdlerization of literary works. Moreover, the dramatic shift in emphasis at the U.S. Department of Education from technology (under Terrel Bell's leadership) to the humanities (under William Bennett's) will keep textbooks and trade books up front for a while. But Bennett's decidedly belletristic focus will have the unintended effect of driving teachers to nonprint modes as a way of expanding the English and language arts curriculum beyond the traditional literary canon—and beyond the even narrower concept of "cultural literacy."[34]

The English class of the long-range future will be characterized by *combinations* of books and other technologies. As the Ryan study shows, we have had some such combinations since the early 1900s, but the ratios apparently shift with the times—and with the fads. I doubt that interactive fiction (an advanced multiple choice/fill-in-the-rhetorical-blanks exercise) will long be confused with the benefits of reading books, but the true power of the videodisc should emerge through as-yet-undeveloped interactive programs that combine print, image, and sound—in children's literature, perhaps, or general semantics.

Print-on-screen will probably outrace textbooks and workbooks that are mere compendia of rules and exercises. As software improves, the computer could be an efficient source of diagnosis and prescription in matters of mechanics, just as math software can now identify "bugs" in students' mathematical skills instead of just telling students that they are right or wrong. I agree with the late Robert Pooley, who said back in 1961 that the computer is probably a good place for exercises and other routine materials. Surely, he argued, the teacher and student must have more interesting things to do than talk about footnote form or absolute phrases.

Even in our larger multimedia environment, the new technologies routinely combine print with visual and auditory images. Commercial TV ads bear names, addresses, and product descriptions. Videotex is among the cable TV options, and we can expect even more words-on-screen as people begin to shop by television. Moreover, the familiar "tie-ins" of books with television programs and movies are being expanded by new tie-ins between books and videodiscs. Print is an integral part of numerous home computer software programs, including many games.

But in the final analysis, English and language arts educators must acknowledge that most new technologies are for the most part best suited for intensive presentation of nonprint symbol systems. Print snippets linked with aural and visual experiences are not what print literacy is about. Even massive databases that present print-only displays of stock market reports, the latest news, or other such data are essentially information aggregates and not mind-stretching expositions. A forty-character, thirty-four-line monitor is ill-suited to what Roger Brown calls "deep reading."[35] Extended essays, short stories, and novels are texts that require reflection and lead to synthesis of knowledge, to real insight rather than mere intake. I believe that the book will remain the preferred medium for developing higher-order thinking abilities and that the classroom will be the training ground for intensive and extensive interchange of ideas among students and their teachers. Finally, the packaging of ideas in books gives to human beings *experiences* and *feelings* that video screens, slide/tape shows, and other media cannot ultimately replace.

Notes

1. C. F. Grenier, "Hook Up, Plug In, Connect: Relevancy Is All," *English Journal* 58 (1969): 23–29; and A. R. Mangione, "The Times They Are A'Changing?" *Elementary English* 48 (1971): 703–4.
2. J. Dixon, *Growth through English* (Reading, England: National Association for the Teaching of English, 1967), 113.
3. M. Griffith and E. Seidman, review of *Understanding Media,* by Marshall McLuhan, *College Composition and Communication* 19 (1968): 72.
4. Sally Zakariya, "The Computer Goes to School," *Principal* 61 (May 1982): 18–19.

5. "Footnotes," *Chronicle of Higher Education,* 8 June 1981, 17.
6. Quoted in Pamela Camerra Rowe, "New Technology Could Go the Way of Instructional Television, Educator Says," *Education Daily,* 25 January 1985, 6.
7. Dan Lacy, "Print, Television, Computers, and English," *ADE Bulletin,* Summer 1982, 34–38.
8. Frederick Erickson, "School Literacy, Reasoning, and Civility: An Anthropologist's Perspective," *Review of Educational Research* 54, no. 4 (1984): 525–46.
9. For a fuller explication of the ideas on the chart, see Geraldine Johncich Clifford, "Buch und Lesen: Historical Perspectives on Literacy," *Review of Educational Research* 54, no. 4 (1984): 472–500, and Charles Suhor, "The Role of Print as a Medium in Our Society," in *Becoming Readers in a Complex Society,* 1984 Yearbook of the National Society for the Study of Education, ed. A. Purves and O. Niles (Chicago: Univ. of Chicago Press, 1984), 20–24.
10. The period 1912–1960 was studied by T. Ryan, who examined attitudes toward media in secondary English as revealed in the *English Journal.* His report shows that the subject of media in the English program was hotly controversial in the decades before the McLuhan revolution. Although *English Journal* writers approved of mass media in the English classroom by a ratio of six to one, such study was attacked vigorously by many writers who feared that the new media were purveyors of immorality and a threat to the nation's intellectual standards. Some writers believed that media should be studied and used only by students incapable of dealing with regular English programs. See T. Ryan, "Mass Media in the Secondary School: An Examination of the Attitudes of the National Council of Teachers of English, 1912–1960, toward Five Selected Mass Media as Expressed in *The English Journal*" (Ph.D. dissertation, Ball State University, 1961).
11. Harold S. Broudy, "How Basic Is Aesthetic Education? Or Is 'rt the Fourth R?" *Language Arts* 54 (1977): 631–37; Frank Smith, "The Uses of Language," *Language Arts* 54 (1977): 638–44; Nancy Thompson, "Multi-Media Linguistics," *English Journal* 67 (1978): 104–7; and D. T. Wolfe and R. W. Reising, "Politics and English Teaching, or (Can, Should, Will) We Teach the *Whole* Brain?" *English Journal* 67 (1978): 29–32.
12. J. Moffett and B. J. Wagner, *Student-Centered Language Arts and Reading, K–13* (Boston: Houghton Mifflin, 1976); and James Morrow and Murray Suid, *Media and the Kids* (Rochelle Park, N. J.: Hayden, 1977).
13. R. V. Barry, "Media Use in Nationally Selected High School Programs: A Survey of Secondary School Principals, Department Chairmen, and English Teachers" (Ph.D. diss., Columbia University Teachers College, 1977); Kenneth Donelson, "Uses, Non-Uses, Mis-Uses, Abuses—Media in Arizona English Classes," *Arizona English Bulletin* 12 (1970): 15–30; and A. J. Roberts, "A Study of the Use of Electronic Media by Secondary Language Arts Teachers in the Denver Metropolitan Area" (Ph.D. diss., University of Kansas, 1978).
14. James Squire and Roger Applebee, *High School English Instruction Today* (New York: Appleton-Century-Crofts, 1968).
15. Richard E. Clark, "Reconsidering Research on Learning from Media," *Review of Educational Research* 53 (1983): 445–49.

16. See Gavriel Saloman, *Interaction of Media, Cognition and Learning* (San Francisco: Jossey Bass, 1979).
17. Michael D. Petrovich and Robert D. Tennyson, "Clark's 'Learning from Media': A Critique," *Educational Communication and Technology Journal* 32, no. 4 (1984): 233–41.
18. Henry J. Becker, *School Uses of Microcomputers: Reports from a National Survey,* no. 6 (Baltimore: Johns Hopkins University, 1984).
19. National Education Association, "A Teacher Survey NEA Report: Computers in the Classroom" (Washington, D.C.: National Education Association, 1983).
20. NEA Educational Computer Service, *The Yellow Book of Computer Products for Education,* vol. 2. (Washington, D.C.: National Education Association, 1985); and "Educational Software Advice: Raise Quality, Reduce Number," *Education Daily,* 22 March 1985, 4.
21. W. Patrick Dickson, "Thought-Provoking Software: Juxtaposing Symbol Systems," *Educational Researcher* 14 (1985): 30–38.
22. Colette Daiute, "Issues in Using Computers to Socialize the Writing Process," *Educational Communications and Technology Journal* 33, no. 1 (1985): 41–50.
23. Diane Rothenberg, "On Children and Computers," *Micro Notes* 5, no. 1 (1984): 1–4.
24. National Assessment of Educational Progress, *Write/Rewrite: An Assessment of Revision Skills* (Denver: Education Commission of the States, 1977).
25. Holly O'Donnell, "Teaching Teachers to Use Computers," *English Education* 17, no. 1 (1985): 54–61.
26. For interesting commentaries and summaries of pertinent research, see Lillie Bridwell et al., "The Writing Process and the Writing Machine: Current Research on Word Processors Relevant to the Teaching of Composition," in *New Directions in Composition Research,* ed. R. Beach and L. Bridwell (New York: Guilford Press, 1984); and Daiute, "Issues in Using Computers."
27. See, for example, IRA Computer Technology and Reading Committee, "Guidelines for Educators on Using Computers in the Schools," *Reading Research Quarterly* 20, no. 1 (Fall 1984): 120–22; NCTE Committee on Instructional Technology, *Guidelines for Review and Evaluation of English Language Arts Software* (Urbana, Ill.: National Council of Teachers of English, 1984); and NEA Educational Computer Service, *The Yellow Book,* vol. 2.
28. Samuel Howe, "Interactive Video: Salt-and-Pepper Technology," *Media & Methods,* January 1985, 8–12.
29. "TVs and Computers Pair Up," *Advance,* Winter 1985, 3, 6–7.
30. Betsy S. Barber, "Technological Change and English Teaching: A Delphi Study of American, British, and Canadian English Educators' Views of the Future of Secondary English Teaching" (Department of Curriculum and Instruction, University of Connecticut, typescript, 1985).
31. "Videodiscs Liven Reading Classes in New York School," *Education Computer News,* 24 April 1985, 1–4.
32. Mark Lewyn, "Take a Letter: $6,500 Device Has a 1,000-Word Vocabulary," *USA Today,* 23 April 1985, 1–13.

33. "Video Conference Slow to Catch On," *USA Today,* 10 January 1985, 68.
34. See E. D. Hirsch, "'Cultural Literacy' Doesn't Mean 'Core Curriculum,'" *English Journal* 74, no. 6 (1985): 47–49.
35. Roger Brown, "The Three *Moonrakers*: An Inquiry into Communication Potentials of Different Media" (Address at the Annual Convention of the National Council of Teachers of English, San Francisco, 22–24 November 1979).

III Change: Toward 2011

10 The Political Issues since 1960

Miriam T. Chaplin

According to the 1983–84 edition of the *Digest of Educational Statistics,* there were 2.2 million classroom teachers in 1981; of these more than 51,000 were teachers of English. Because students are required to study the English language and/or literature at every level of schooling through the sophomore year of college, English departments often constitute as much as 25 percent of an institution's teaching faculty. It is often said that as the English department goes, so goes the faculty. But the importance of English teachers stems not from the size of the profession, but from its mission.

Speaking at an NCTE College Section Meeting in 1965, Richard Ohmann identified the goal of the English profession as "the fostering of literary culture and literary consciousness."[1] Ohmann's concise and accurate statement of professional objectives is applicable to English teachers regardless of their assignment. These objectives distinguish English teachers from all other teachers. But they also place English teachers in the vanguard of the changes and challenges that confront the teaching profession generally, since the fostering of literacy embraces all disciplines. Indeed, language competence is the bedrock of all education, meaning that English teachers bear a heavy responsibility for students' academic development—and thus are quite vulnerable to attack. If students do not exhibit acceptable reading and writing skills, it is assumed that English teachers are at least partly at fault. Despite recent efforts to spread the responsibility for language teaching across the curriculum, English teachers remain the chief agents for education in literacy. Since the promulgation of literacy is fundamental to change and advancement in this as in all modern industrial societies, the effect of national and world events on education is especially felt by English teachers.

Since the birth of NCTE in 1911, American education has been affected by a host of social, economic, and political events: economic depression, recession, and growth; atomic destruction and threats of nuclear annihilation; military conflicts and cold wars; the intense efforts of various groups to attain social, political, and economic equality; political assassinations and scandals; diversity in personal morals and values; international arms races and attempts at disarmament; immense preoccupation with outer space; a technical revolution; and a near-collapse of the two-party system in American politics. The educational system has responded by restructuring curricula, providing opportunities for local communities to participate in the process of education, instituting standards of teacher accountability, fostering increased sensitivity toward population diversity, unionizing teachers, establishing standards for student achievement, and using monitoring devices to evaluate student performance.

The level of teaching assignment and specific institutional characteristics cause differences in the way English teachers react to an ever-changing world. Elementary teachers in self-contained public classrooms may not respond like high school teachers, and high school teachers have different challenges than those of junior college or four-year college and university teachers. English teachers assigned to private schools and penal institutions as well as teachers who work in the business, health, or legal professions must conform to the standards and unique settings of those institutions. While all English teachers are affected by society's changes and challenges, the level and intensity of their reactions are situation-specific. Within the last twenty-five years, there have been four issues that have had particularly important impact on the English profession. Accordingly, much of NCTE's attention has been directed to them. They are: equal access, unionization, teacher accountability, and censorship. All English teachers, regardless of their assignment, have been touched in some way by at least one of these issues.

Equal Access

The first NCTE meeting was held nine years before passage of the Nineteenth Amendment, forty-three years before *Brown vs. Topeka,* fifty-three years before the 1964 Civil Rights Act, sixty-one years before Title IX, and sixty-four years before PL 94–142. The civil rights actions affirmed the basic rights of blacks, handicapped individuals, other minorities, and women to equal access to institutions of their choice. As a result of this legislation and the birth of affirmative action, most institutions made concerted efforts to fill available teaching positions with qualified minorities and women. At the same time, student bodies in high schools and colleges also changed. Population shifts within the nation and the increased immigration of people from the Far and Middle Eastern part of the world as well as from the lands and islands to the south of the continental United States increased the racial diversity of students. Women became a majority of the college population in the 1970s and 1980s. By 1990 in several states, including Texas, California, New York, and New Jersey, minorities will make up approximately 35 percent of the graduating high school seniors.[2] Thus, while some predict a decline in college populations generally, the numbers of minorities in higher education may remain constant or even increase.

The initial influx of this diversified student population demanded faculty who could identify with the students' unique experiences and learning styles. It was soon realized, however, that the hiring of such faculty alone was not sufficient to meet the needs of the students. More substantive changes in the scope of the curriculum and in instructional approaches were required. Since the students represented different ethnic origins and nationalities and many had suffered the consequences of racial discrimination and/or poverty, they needed historical references on which they could build positive self-images. To accommodate this need, high schools and colleges broadened the traditional English curriculum of American and European literature to include minority literature and literature by and about women. The problems of self-image were compounded, however, by the fact that many of these students came from varying linguistic backgrounds and their facility with standard forms of written and spoken English was considered by educational institutions to be below acceptable levels.

To correct these alleged deficiencies, "remedial" writing courses with heavy concentrations of instruction in grammar were instituted; nevertheless, students held tenaciously to the variations of the language which were a part of their heritage. Teachers soon discovered that writing practice rather than grammar drills was the key to students' development. That practice, however, had to be reality-based instead of superficial academic exercises such as those James Britton refers to as "dummy runs." Britton says that students "must practice language as a lawyer practices law and not in the sense in which a juggler practices a new trick before he performs it."[3]

Within the large group of nontraditional students, there were many subgroups. One group included mature men and women returning to school to pursue a second career or to finish an interrupted education. These mature students were interested in the future, but they were also interested in using their education to reflect upon past experiences. They did not adapt to lecture classes in which the instructor's view and those of his or her selected references were paramount. These students called for interactive class discussions in which they could use their personal experiences in life as a reference in applying newly acquired knowledge.

English teachers were not especially equipped by their training to comply with demands for instruction in oral and written composition. Prior to the 1960s, the educational preparation of English teachers focused almost exclusively on literature, with only a cursory attention to the teaching of writing. In some institutions, courses in linguistics were mandated, but sociolinguistics, knowledge crucial to effective instruction for this new student population, was rarely a required course. Traditionally, the format for college English instruction was the lecture, and students in English had continued to use their professors as models for their own teaching behaviors. Not only did these nontraditional students reject traditional teaching behaviors, however, they also insisted on fundamental changes in the content and structure of the discipline.

Heavy teaching schedules and assignments beyond their areas of expertise created additional difficulties for teachers. Many high school teachers were assigned as many as six classes per day. Despite their limited training in teaching writing, high school teachers and junior college teachers as well as junior faculty at the four-year colleges either taught composition exclusively or along with lower-level literature classes. There were widespread complaints about class size and the impossibility of individualizing instruction. English teachers were assigned to teach courses in reading, study skills, and life skills, or they became the coordinators of writing and reading laboratories that had been created to fill the gaps in students' skill levels. Furthermore, in some instances, particularly in the high schools, the teachers had trouble getting students' attention and maintaining order. Many students were either apathetic or hostile to the teachers' efforts. These students were the products of ability grouping, remedial instruction, and other methods which served to label students as chronic underachievers. The apathetic students withdrew and resigned themselves to the stigma that surrounded them; the hostile students struck out at the teachers whom they believed to be representatives of institutions that had failed them.

Teachers who turned to the professional journals and associations for assistance discovered that the English profession generally was also in the midst of change. Spurred by the Dartmouth Conference in 1966 and its emphasis on a personal growth model, and followed by Janet Emig's study of the *Composing Processes of Twelfth Graders* in 1971, the profession was beginning to shift its attention away from the product of written discourse to the process that writers use in production. James Moffett published his *Teaching the Universe of Discourse* in 1968 with its accompanying *Student-Centered Language Arts Curriculum, Grades K–13.* These texts provided innovative alternatives to traditional classroom methods and offered a theory of instruction as well. The Schools Council Project on Writing Across the Curriculum was being conducted in England. In many graduate schools, students were being introduced to the work of L. S. Vygotsky, Jean Piaget, and Jerome Bruner and the relationship of this research to English education. Mina Shaughnessy was conducting research with her basic writing students at the City University of New York in an attempt to explain the anatomy of error in basic writing courses. These were exciting times for the professionally alert teacher. Yet there were those who were so overwhelmed by the breadth of their immediate tasks that they simply could not collect the strength to look about them.

Whether the renaissance in the English profession grew because of the new student population or in spite of it is difficult to say. We know certainly, however, that all students have benefited from the reforms in English education since 1960.

Women and minorities of color, age, and national origin had entered college communities in numbers larger than ever before. These students were accused of lowering academic standards, but their presence raised teachers' sensitivities. Because this new generation of students gained access, the educational establishment would never be the same again.

Teacher Accountability

Parents and the general public have always held English teachers accountable for the educational progress of children because success in formal schooling is so closely associated with literacy. The issue of teacher accountability, however, became especially prominent in the 1970s. The two factors responsible for this renewed emphasis were the influence of business practices on education and the increased participation of local communities in school affairs. The media spread reports of widespread functional illiteracy among high school students and a decline in the college board scores of students seeking college admission. In the face of this alleged inadequate preparation of students and increased federal and state appropriations to education, the indignation of the public was aroused to the point of demanding that teachers justify their output (students' qualifications) in terms of the input (public monies).

While mathematics was also considered crucial, the attack on math teachers was somehow less specific than on English teachers, and teachers in the disciplines outside of English and mathematics shielded themselves with the popular excuse that they couldn't teach content if students couldn't read, write, or compute. The primacy of these skills was validated by the state departments of education, many of which ordered competency testing to identify students' skill levels in reading, writing, and mathematics ability only. Furthermore, the tests, objective in format, could measure only a set of narrowly isolated skills in these areas. Since the scores from the tests were reported in terms of grade, school, and district where the tests were administered, the teachers of low-achieving students could easily be targeted. Thus despite the fact that the English profession was calling for more attention to personal writing and the composing process, teachers were being compelled to direct instruction to the narrow skills that the tests measured.

Elementary teachers were no more able than high school or college teachers to apply the theories of English education they were learning in graduate courses or through professional literature. Like teachers at the higher levels, those in the elementary grades were expected to teach reading and writing skills in a way most expedient to success in testing situations. Therefore, in many classrooms rote learning was more prevalent than approaches consistent with the reforms in the profession. The "back to basics" movement became primarily a testing movement and did not lead to the improvement it sought.

Largely because of this lack of success, the dawn of the 1980s brought an ideological shift from education aimed at students' attainment of basic skills or minimum competencies to an emphasis on teachers' proficiency in these skill areas. Another reason for the change in focus was the reduction of appropriations to finance remedial programs for students. Less expensive and more lasting approaches to competency needed to be considered. Again, the media led the way in turning the public's attention toward new targets. The newspapers and magazines that had reported students' low test scores began to say that Johnny couldn't read and Jenny couldn't write because teachers couldn't teach, and that teachers couldn't teach because they couldn't read or write much better than could Johnny or Jenny. The accusations of incompetence were not aimed specifically at English teachers but at all teachers. This kind of reporting, however, proved to be especially embarrassing to English teachers because literacy was their stock-in-trade. Nevertheless, the issue gained national attention and the nation embarked on an era of reform.

Teacher-certification programs in colleges and universities were reviewed by state departments of education and the decision to institute competency tests for teacher applicants became widespread. "One of the fastest-moving changes in this piece of educational reform is in teacher testing. In as little as five years, state-required testing for aspiring teachers to enter preparation and/or become certified has spread from a handful of states—mainly in the Southeast—to a nationwide trend involving 38 states, with seven additional states currently considering a teacher testing requirement. In 1984 alone, nine states enacted teacher testing laws or regulations."[4]

A review of the scores of applicants who have taken these tests reveal that minorities score lower than whites. The test used most often is the National Teachers' Examination, which contains a variety of subtests called Specialty Area Tests, one being English Language and Literature. According to a survey of scores compiled by the Educational Testing Service in 1985, the mean score for white applicants taking the English Language and Literature test was 603 while the mean score for black applicants was 470. Hispanics and other minorities are not included in this analysis.[5]

These figures are important because many of these teacher applicants were students who came to college as a result of the equal access legislation and who matriculated during a period of great change and upheaval in the English profession. English departments in many institutions are just beginning to adjust curricula to reflect new advances; others continue to resist. Therefore, the incompetencies that the tests are revealing in minority teacher applicants may more accurately show the failure of the traditional English curriculum to meet the needs of a diverse student population than they indicate that minorities are inherently inferior prospects for teaching careers. Of course, it is also disturbing to realize that teacher-competency testing, regardless of the underlying reason, is reducing the number of minority teachers at a time when minority student populations continue to increase. Since the reduction will lead to fewer role models for students, there may be a resurgence of the self-image problems experienced by minority students a decade ago.

The accountability movement is destined to be a central concern for several years. Unless it creates an impetus for a change in education that results in the development of teachers who can use the English language with confidence, imagination, and sensitivity, it will represent one more period in American education that commands much attention but does not reform.

Unionization

Few issues in education have attracted as much attention as the subject of unionization and collective bargaining. Most teachers would agree that collective bargaining has helped them to obtain benefits that individual efforts could never have obtained. Yet some of these same teachers complain about the tactics that unions use to win concessions. While salary and fringe benefits are the areas in which collective bargaining has been most beneficial to teachers, the unions have affected the careers of English teachers in other ways equally important to their professional standing.

Foremost among the accomplishments of collective bargaining favoring English teachers at the high school level has been increased equity in extracurricular assignments. Prior to collective bargaining, English teachers were often simply assigned ancillary tasks such as advising the debating team or drama club or coaching oratorical and essay contests or spelling bees. These assignments were in addition to teachers' regular duties and without financial compensation. While some teachers enjoyed the extracurricular involvement, they admitted that these duties were often thankless impositions on their personal time. English teachers still serve in such roles, but where there is a functioning union, the contract usually forbids assignment without permission. When teachers agree to work beyond the school day, they are often compensated at an hourly rate.

Teachers' contracts have also limited the number of classes that high school English teachers may be assigned and have set limits on class size as well. To be able to teach writing effectively, English teachers must work individually with students in conferences or small groups, and the smaller the class, the more workable and effective these sessions can be. Smaller classes and reduced teaching loads also allow English teachers the opportunity to spend more time assessing students' progress in writing and communicating with students about strengths and needs.

Higher education has not escaped the union movement, though college unions have not received as much media attention as those in lower levels. There are reasons for the differences, both intrinsically and in the public perception. First, faculty governance and academic freedom are essential ingredients of the professoriate. Many of the issues that have consumed the energies of public and private school unions are not negotiable in higher education because they are handled through peer review. Second, strikes appear to be more disruptive in the lower grades because the students are at the ages of compulsory schooling. They are moving up through the grades in order to attend college or to enter the workforce. When teachers' strikes interfere with this process, parents become annoyed and openly display their anger. The media has capitalized on scenes of teachers on picket lines engaging in shouting matches with parents. College students, on the other hand, are considered adults. They do not depend on the intervention of parents for their welfare—nor so directly on the property taxes parents pay—and so college unions do not arouse the public controversy that unions do at lower levels.

Unions representing college professors have bargained successfully for higher salaries and fringe benefits, and they have defended faculty in promotion and tenure cases. Unions and professional organizations have not been especially vocal, however, in two issues of special importance to English teachers at the college level—the reassignment of faculty tenured in other disciplines to English departments and the hiring of temporary and part-time faculty.

The general decline in college populations and the popularity of business and computer science as major courses of study have reduced the number of students seeking majors in the humanities, the arts, and the social sciences. The composition requirement in college curricula has helped English departments to maintain healthy class loads. Other disciplines do not have such broad-based requirements. Yet they may have faculty at the senior ranks who must be protected even when the student population decreases, and some college administrators consider reassignment to be a viable alternative. Hence, they assign professors in the low-enrollment disciplines to English departments, where they are expected to teach writing. In some cases, the institutions require that such reassigned faculty attend training classes to prepare them for the new assignment. These training sessions are often hurriedly instituted and do not contain the in-depth preparation necessary for effective instruction. Therefore, reassignment is not viewed favorably by college English teachers because (1) it deprives well-trained teachers of employment opportunities at a time when jobs are scarce and (2) it supports the view that anyone can teach writing—a myth that English teachers feel is unfair, untrue, and insulting.

The hiring of temporary and part-time faculty is another issue of interest to college English teachers. Because federal and state allocations to higher education have steadily declined in recent years, institutions have become reluctant to increase their numbers of tenure-track positions, and the hiring of temporary and part-time faculty to teach writing courses has become a popular practice. While it may be argued that this at least provides employment for English graduates in a severely depressed market, the practice is exploitative. Faculty hired under temporary conditions are not included in the benefits negotiated for full-time faculty. The institution makes no commitment for their continued employment, and often they exist without the necessary conveniences that other college faculty enjoy, such as office space and travel allowances to attend professional meetings. Moreover, they are confined to such lower-division courses as freshman writing, reading/writing laboratories, and remedial/developmental courses.

Reassignment and temporary appointments are issues which strike at the heart of the English professoriate. In which discipline are reassigned professors expected to publish? And by which colleagues will their work be reviewed and promotion decisions made? If temporary faculty are not eligible for faculty research support, will this stifle their motivation to contribute to knowledge in their field? These are questions that threaten the stability, mobility, and productivity of college faculties now and in the future, and should concern unions that bargain in favor of college teachers.

Censorship

Public schools are expected to represent the ideals on which our government rests. Since free speech and free thought are fundamental concepts in a democracy, they should be an integral part of all public education in America. Thus argue those who oppose censorship of books and instructional materials. But consistent and logical arguments aside, the question of which values are to be championed during the educational process is complex and involves a whole range of variables that get in the way of a simple answer. The censorship issue is religious, political, moral, economic, ethnic, and cultural. Rarely is a position based on only one of these considerations; it is more often a combination of factors derived from personal experiences and idiosyncracies.

Censorship is not a new phenomenon in education. Forces beyond the school have always attempted to influence the kinds of materials used to instruct students. In the last two decades, however, censorship has become more intense and pervasive. For English teachers, this has been especially troubling and constraining because we have been charged with the responsibility of teaching the literature of the past and the present. When teachers are inhibited in their choice of materials, their freedoms are placed in jeopardy. The freedom of students is equally imperiled, since the right to read refers not only to learning how to engage in the process, but to the exercise of choice as well. The manuscripts writers release for publication belong to the world. Copyright laws will protect their duplication, but nothing should interfere with any individual's right to read and interpret them. It is not, then, surprising that one of the most popular NCTE publications in the last two decades has been the pamphlet *The Student's Right to Read*.

The censorship issue affects more than the teaching of literature in the English classroom. Writing in *English Journal,* John S. Simmons refers to the tremendous impact that censorship is having on the publication industry. Fearing that books with any controversial ideas will be banned, publishers censor their own authors prior to publication. This sterilization of ideas results in the publication of materials void of anything provocative. According to Simmons,

> the new brand of censorship hits English teachers at a critical moment in their careers. Can they lead students to an awareness of cultural relativism in the study of dialect and usage, or is it back to Warriner's and surrender to basic backwardness? Can they do an honest job with general semantics, using advertising and propaganda techniques as illustrations, or will that run counter to the need to promote the American Way? And what can be done about the choosing of literary works that represent the demise of the Western World in the second half of the twentieth century? . . . In the first place, the need to promote *critical* reading among secondary school students is becoming more and more evident. Large numbers of school students appear to be limited in ability to draw inferences, make judgments, arrive at conclusions and test hypotheses as they read. . . . But the prohibitive nature of the new wave of censorship may well deny publication of engagingly written materials about pressing issues.[6]

Melvin and Norma Gabler have been in the forefront of the new censorship. These two Texans have reviewed hundreds of books and successfully waged campaigns to have many of them banned. The rise of the Moral Majority and its insistence on an orthodox Christian and narrowly patriotic viewpoint has also helped to influence parents, community groups, and legislators to prohibit the circulation and reading of books conservative groups deem inappropriate for developing minds. Though there has been a proliferation of private schools organized by sympathizers of such movements as the Moral Majority, these groups continue to use their influence to control reading materials in public schools as well.

Censorship, however, has not been exercised by conservatives alone. Liberals have also played an active role in having books removed from library shelves and school book closets. One of their targets has been the elimination of racial stereotyping. As a result, Dick and Jane, Puff and Spot, who live in a little white suburban house with a picket fence, have gone the way of Sambo and of "red savages" talking in monosyllables. While stereotyping is usually thought to inhibit the objective thought processes that teachers try to foster, anticensorship conservatives contend that liberal censorship is no less harmful than any other.

In the atmosphere of the new censorship, no book is sacrosanct—one line or phrase may be enough to cause the alarm of parents and other community leaders. English teachers who refuse to conform to the new censorship jeopardize their careers. Those who believe that such interferences into their professional judgments are dehumanizing either leave the profession or never enter at all.

Facing the Challenge

Martin Buber once said: "Experience comes to man as 'I,' but it is by experience as 'we' that he builds the common world in which he lives."[7] NCTE is at the core of the professional world of English teachers. A review of the resolutions, position statements, and publications of the council shows the breadth of its involvement in the concerns of the English profession. These statements have originated in extended discussions within the committees, commissions, task forces, and caucuses of NCTE and its affiliates. Therefore, NCTE is an avenue through which English teachers can discover the collective "we" to which Buber refers and use the group voice to respond to the changes and challenges that confront them.

A jubilee celebration is a time for reflection, but it is also a time for commitment—a time for rededication to the principles that have emerged from lessons of the past. English teachers have learned much about teaching and learning. They have learned to view students' writing as much as a means of self-discovery as an act of affirmation or denial of selected topics and issues. Research has revealed that language plays a key role in the process of learning. Theories of reading are fostering the idea that students should read for self-fulfillment and personal interpretations. More English teachers are teaching with their ears tuned to students' individual rhythms and are allowing students to march to the beat of their own drummers. These lessons have been learned in the classrooms, graduate schools, and professional meetings, and through personal experiences. Yet there are other lessons that must be learned—lessons that are not directly related to teaching and learning.

English teachers must assume more responsibility for their own destinies. For too long, teachers have allowed public outcry to determine directions that education should pursue. Legislators rather than educators have pointed out the need for reform, and therefore complex problems have given rise to simple solutions that are often politically based and not educationally sound. These kinds of actions will continue until teachers seize more securely the reins of their profession and use peripheral vision to look about them and extended vision to look ahead. English teachers must gaze at the landscape of their profession and find the hills to build on and the hillocks to level out. They must use available resources to attain carefully planned goals and point to their successes to prove the need for additional resources.

The controversies surrounding the issues of equal access, accountability, unionization, and censorship, along with countless others, will continue to challenge the profession. Through individual commitment and group efforts, English teachers can turn these roadblocks into stepping stones to a more secure future.

Notes

1. Richard Ohmann, speech at 1965 College Section Meeting of the National Council of Teachers of English, published in *English in America: A Radical View of the Profession* (New York: Oxford Univ. Press, 1976), 13.
2. Marilyn Schuster and Susan Van Dyne, "Placing Women in the Liberal Arts: Stages of Curriculum Transformation," *Harvard Educational Review* 54, no. 4 (Nov. 1984): 413–14.
3. James Britton, *Language and Learning* (Baltimore, Md.: Penguin, 1972), 130.
4. Gregory R. Anrig, "Teacher Education and Teacher Testing: The Rush to Mandate," Research Report for Educational Testing Service, 1985, 1.
5. Margaret E. Goertz, "The Impact of NTE Use by States on Teacher Selection," Research Report for Educational Testing Service, 1985, 23.
6. John S. Simmons, "Proactive Censorship," *English Journal* 70, no. 8 (Dec. 1981): 20.
7. Martin Buber, *Between Man and Man* (London: Routledge & Kegan Paul, 1947), 46.

11 Imperatives for the Future

James R. Squire

The major curriculum reform movements of the past half century have concentrated either on achieving excellence for academically able students or on achieving equity for the economically deprived or culturally diverse. So it was during the school reform movement of the first decades of the century when NCTE was founded, when great waves of new Americans required a basic adjustment of the common school curriculum to provide equal opportunity for many new immigrant groups. So it was during the last great academic reform movement of the fifties and early sixties, when teaching "new" mathematics, sciences, foreign languages, and "tripod English" for the college-bound circumscribed our interest in school reform. And so it was in the mid-sixties and early seventies, when urban school reform, inevitably awakened by the nation's social conscience, focused on providing equal educational opportunities for the disadvantaged. Never in history have we attempted to achieve both excellence and equity as we must today.

These continuing issues, still largely unresolved, remain with us: academic "softness," lack of concern with subject matter, the slighting of the gifted and talented, yet, also, programs unsuited to the new Americans, for example the millions of Hispanics and Asians, or programs that fail to respond to differences created by economic and ethnic discrimination. Even as this is written, a new national reform commission in *Barriers to Excellence: Our Children at Risk* warns that too many of today's proposed reforms will not provide excellence in education for at least 25 percent of our children. If today's English reform movement is to provide a strong, continuing impetus toward achieving both excellence and equity in education, then at least *seven* conditions must be met.

1. Literacy must be redefined.

Excellence in English instruction means excellence for all. No single Procrustean standard can be established to define achievement in language and literature. Standards there must be for all—high expectations and support in striving toward these expectations for young people in every economic, cultural, and academic group. But the diversity of our student population will not yield to uniform grade and age-level requirements.

Particularly distressing in the current scene are the various popular definitions of literacy that seem to equate the minimal competencies needed in language with age/grade word lists or simplistic readability formulas designed for different purposes. We need to recognize that reading and writing are becoming more important in our technological age and that citizens who soon must transmit messages electronically and instantaneously require skills and competencies far more advanced than those currently seen at the threshold of literacy. Further, should not our concept of literacy be extended to include basic awareness of key cultural documents of our national heritage? Who can, after all, think the thoughts of a Lincoln or a Kennedy or a Martin Luther King, Jr., unless nourished on the same food? *The Book in Our Future,* the new report to the Congress from the Center for the Book, stresses this need for a common literacy. More sharply focused attention, then, to both the ends and the essence of English becomes a hallmark of excellence in education.

2. All candidates must have access to the tools of learning and the carriers of our culture.

One of the startling characteristics of the past decade in American education has been our neglect of school libraries and of providing children with ready access to books. Twenty years ago, spurred by federal support for school libraries, education scored major gains in installing libraries in the majority of elementary schools. Yet concern with children's access to books no longer seems a priority. School library budgets do not permit replacement of worn copies; funding for instructional materials has dropped to around 0.8 percent of total school expenditures, about half of the commitment twenty years ago. In our anxiety to install major computer laboratories in our schools, we have neglected the book—our bedrock resource. Teachers of English must see that such resources are restored.

The research is abundantly clear that children who achieve early independence in reading are children who have early access to books—at home, in schools, in preschool settings. Perhaps nothing would do more to stimulate substantial growth for all children in reading and writing in the primary school than increasing tenfold or twentyfold their access to books. This need is particularly critical for children of low socioeconomic status, whose working parents are often unable to provide the needed resources.

3. Stress must be placed on the higher thought processes essential to English.

Curriculum-mapping studies and other research into what is really happening in our classrooms indicate clearly that, insofar as reading and writing are concerned, we overemphasize word-level and sentence-level instruction and neglect the discourse level. Yet almost all of the higher thought processes in composition and in comprehension occur beyond the sentence level. Not only have we found that as much as 90 percent of classroom instruction and practice in reading and language arts occurs at the sentence level or below (at least in grades three to six) but less than 10 percent of class time—in English and in subject classes—allows for student generation of productive language. Unless boys and girls have opportunities to process ideas—through productive language—they are unlikely to learn to think.

More instruction than in reading, writing, and oral interaction seems essential in every discipline. Teaching methodology which emphasizes constructive response to ideas is important at every grade level. The quiet, orderly classroom focusing on skill drills or silent reading is not likely to teach many to think. It takes two to read a book or to complete any act of communication.

The need for interactive educational experience for economically disadvantaged students requires special emphasis in view of the long schoolroom tradition that such students respond best to classrooms circumscribed by coverage of discrete skills, small increments in learning, and ultimately almost complete subservience to word-level, sub-word-level, and sentence-level activity.

4. Technology must be used to strengthen reading, writing, and thinking.

The world of microcomputers and other technological aids offers significant new opportunities to those concerned with the processing of ideas through language, yet only if we think through how to use computers as tools for the mind. Useful as are computers in supporting administrative responsibilities for testing and instructional management or for providing an alternative for print-based drill and practice, technology used in such ways merely replicates what we are already able to do manually.

Where computers are able to contribute substantially to excellence in English is through the uses of word processors. Instructing and guiding practice in the composing process—planning, drafting, editing, publishing—naturally flows from the employment of processors for group writing activities and stimulates interactive learning as well. Interactive comprehension experiences in literature or, for that matter, in history, science, or geography become far more manageable as young people are guided to set purpose in reading activities, activate background knowledge, explore text structure, review connotative meanings, and analyze authors' intent. Recent reviews by the Educational Products Information Exchange suggest that currently the most creative software may be available in social studies. Specialists in language need to direct urgent attention to how these tools for processing language are being employed in English, and especially how they are being used with students of lower socioeconomic status. Recent status studies suggest that not only do children from culturally different and economically handicapped backgrounds have fewer opportunities than their peers to interact with computers, but that what experience they have is more than twice as likely to be limited to drill and practice activity.

5. Tests and textbooks must be strengthened.

The lack of fit of goals, texts, and tests has become one of the major concerns of school reformers during the early eighties. It is about time. We know that what we test affects what is taught and what is learned. To a considerable degree, the lack of attention to the uses of productive language and to constructive response to reading reflects the focus of many state and district assessments and virtually all standardized tests (in all subjects) on sentence-level and word-level skills.

Given the magnitude of the problem the task of changing is enormous. More than seventy different state tests are currently in use. Most program-related textbook examinations reflect the characteristic activities of published instruments (since they exist in part to prepare children for external examinations). Teacher-made tests may be the most deficient of all—albeit the easiest to change.

Needed is greater awareness on the part of all teachers of English of the ramifications of an assessment program and the opportunities implicit in adopting "multiple sloppy measures" to guide instruction, to use a term coined in Pennsylvania. Indeed, awareness of the present need for multiple approaches to evaluation may in itself stimulate excellence in education.

Recent uses of writing samples are important in encouraging employment of interactive computerized instruments to assess growth in the power to think and seem to offer manageable administrative approaches. Those who care the most deeply about the quality of literacy and language education need to step forward with comprehensive assessment programs.

6. Our K–12 programs in literary education must be redefined.

With the sole exception of Mortimer Adler's *Paideia Proposal,* the teaching of literature seems almost neglected in the current spate of reform reports. In one or two important states—particularly in California under the watchful eye of State Superintendent William Honig—the quality of the schools' literary education is receiving serious thought. The newly instituted survey of critical literacy, to involve Diane Ravitch, E. D. Hirsch, and several other of our more insightful critics, promises to alert us to the issues. Too often, however, overt concern with basic reading and writing skills leads unintentionally to a neglect of our common heritage and, quite possibly, to a reduction in the time devoted to literary studies.

Further, the common heritage seems singularly uncommon if graduates from our schools and colleges share few literary experiences. The recent lack of attention to building a common heritage seems singularly inappropriate at a time when researchers in cognitive psychology are demonstrating the power of background knowledge in shaping an individual's capability to understand and respond to what he or she reads. Yet, for many of our students, a common background is unlikely unless created by the school.

Understandably worried about reinstituting prescribed curriculum requirements in reading, few leaders in teaching literature are yet ready to argue even for specifying a small number of titles. As the National Coalition of English Associations stated in mid-1984, "So much excellent literature exists that different schools may reasonably make different selections of literature for the students."

Still, quality must be a factor. We must never let our concern about the literary transaction between book and reader blind us to an awareness that the richness of the transaction is directly related to the quality of the stimulus. We may need to reexamine the literary canon to identify those books which speak to young people today. But we can't ignore our heritage. There may be gaps in any student's literary education, but those gaps should not include all Shakespeare, all Dickens, all writers of the New England Renaissance, all poetry, all great books for children, all Greco-Roman mythology, and the great rhetorical tradition of the democratic peoples.

7. Teaching conditions and teacher education must be reconstituted to support achievement of excellence.

Excellence and equity in English will never be achieved without stronger and more imaginative teacher preparation (including inservice staff development) and improved teaching conditions. Fortunately, these problems are receiving such widespread attention that we seem on the verge of establishing more intelligent career paths, better compensation programs, improved pupil-teacher ratios, and the like. In the teaching of English, however, more concern must be given to qualitative considerations. Recent studies in cognitive psychology have taught us much about metacognition, about learning how to learn. We are beginning to apply these insights to the education of children in reading and writing—clarifying purpose, reviewing progress, understanding process, learning how to learn, developing self-monitoring skills.

Yet these same principles of learning apply equally to the learning of adults, and need to be widely considered in our preservice or inservice programs. Certainly, seminar approaches, involving more interactive learning, are urgently needed in staff development. In a sense, our English education programs, like our instruction for students, remain fixed at "word-level" or "sentence-level" discourse.

Conclusion

These seven conditions may not fully describe all of the current concerns with achieving both excellence and equity. But only to the extent that these conditions are met will the nation's schools be able to provide the quality of educational experience envisaged in current reform efforts.

References

Adler, Mortimer J. *The Paideia Proposal: An Educational Manifesto* (New York: Macmillan, 1982).

Boorstin, Daniel. *The Book in Our Future.* Washington, D.C.: Center for the Book, Library of Congress, 1984.

Barriers to Excellence: Our Children at Risk. Boston: National Coalition of Advocates for Students, 1985.

Chall, Jeanne. *Stages of Reading Development.* New York: McGraw-Hill, 1983.

College Entrance Examination Board. *Academic Preparation for College.* New York: College Entrance Examination Board, 1983.

Pearson, P. David, ed. *Handbook of Research in Reading.* New York: Longmans, 1984.

12 NCTE Presidents: Priorities for the Future

Nancy S. McHugh
Sheila Fitzgerald
Richard Lloyd-Jones
Stephen N. Tchudi

In the following roundtable discussion the 1984–86 NCTE presidential team of Nancy McHugh (Grant High School, Van Nuys, California), Sheila Fitzgerald (Michigan State University), Richard Lloyd-Jones (University of Iowa), and Stephen Tchudi (Michigan State University) address problems facing the English teaching profession, suggest priorities, and make some predictions as NCTE enters the quarter century leading to its centennial.

Question: What do you see as the most pressing economic and social issues facing teachers of English and the language arts?

McHugh: We are now involved in a wave of immigration as great as the movement of 1911. Most immigrants are convinced of the necessity and desirability of learning English, yet most do not want to give up their own language. Most have "bought" the American dream, yet most do not want to lose or subvert their own cultural heritage. The "salad" rather than the "melting pot" has been generally accepted by both immigrants and fair-minded citizens of longer standing. NCTE should continue to promote proficiency in English as a key to literacy, social and professional mobility, and participation in the American "experiment," while at the same time affirming the value and psychological necessity of respecting the native language and culture of those culturally diverse and/or more recently settled citizens and inhabitants. For students who are struggling with personal identity at the same time they are acquiring social identity, this fairness policy becomes particularly important.

Lloyd-Jones: The nineteenth century could afford the luxury of forcing the children of immigrants to learn English and let the parents languish, if necessary. At worst there was a great need for docile, unskilled labor.

Today we can neither ignore the parents nor tyrannize the children. Public needs require that everyone have the chance to acquire basic competence in the dominant language—English—but they also require that people acquire knowledge in whatever language they have and take pride in multilanguage competence. There is no need to assume that retaining effectiveness in one's first language eliminates the development of skills in a second or third language.

Language is always political because it is a social instrument tuned to individual and subgroup taste. Political and economic divisions and quarrels become quarrels about "correct" language. English teachers will always have the problem of being referees in such contests. Literature by its nature is unsettling, challenging. Although some texts represent local or national values, most represent elaborations or challenges disturbing to some part of the school patrons, and the teachers who offer the materials for examination will be caught in the middle. Yet it would betray our study if we did not present these challenges even though we must have the tact and gentleness to present the questions without disrupting the basic social fabric.

The better part of the twentieth century has been devoted to developing a system of mass education in schools. For only twenty years or so, however, have we tried to extend that system of mass education beyond high school. Most colleges have not yet adjusted to the bureaucracy, muddled values, and loss of community which has resulted.

Fitzgerald: Many colleges and universities have an increasing number of foreign students on campus, enriching the potential for cultural exchange, new friendships, and world understanding. Problems arise for foreign students in their studies, however, that are not being adequately addressed, including the problems foreign education majors may have understanding the professional concerns of American teachers, the frequent difficulties in student-professor communication about the subtleties of pedagogical matters even when the student has an adequate proficiency in English as his or her second language, the possible inappropriateness of American pedagogies in other cultures, and the problems foreign students sometimes have in writing papers for advanced courses or doctoral dissertations. The needs of the foreign student and the problems of professors who work with foreign students have had little attention in the professional community.

Tchudi: This whole area of multiculturalism and multilingualism is one of enormous opportunity and challenge to the English teaching profession. Ironically, it is also an area we can probably choose to ignore for the simple reason that, despite the public's claimed interest in pluralistic, democratic education, the schools have long been geared to best serve the interests of the "American" majority. Granted, some teachers will inevitably wind up teaching classes that consist of more and more non-native English speakers. Yet those classes can easily enough be assigned to new teachers, aides, and even part-time teachers, while the teaching majority continues with the relative luxury of classes filled with native speakers and writers. I hope that our profession will not ignore the second-language question, and I believe that NCTE can provide significant leadership. We should form closer ties with organizations like Teachers of English to Speakers of Other Languages, but we should also work within our own membership to develop better and better strategies for integrating the needs, interests, and skills of second-language learners in all English classrooms.

Question: Are there domestic issues besides multilingualism that you see as priorities?

Fitzgerald: The inequities among groups of people in our country in securing the necessities of daily life, in gaining access to the refinements of life, and in having job opportunities seem to become more apparent with each passing decade. Children cannot learn well in school if they do not have enough to eat, stable relationships with adults, a vision of their future, and hope for future jobs. Of course, the ultimate need is freedom from fear of annihilation. Control of armaments escalation is essential, therefore, followed by a redirecting of tax money into quality social welfare programs that are as unencumbered by government bureaucracy and restrictive regulations as possible.

McHugh: Decreased funding for education is a national disgrace. The short-sighted, cavalier attitude of "people at the top" is dangerous and reprehensible.

Fitzgerald: One particular type of program that is sorely needed, one that might become an adjunct to school programs, is parent training. Nothing is more basic to the future than parenthood, and nothing is more neglected in our school programs. It seems ironic that driver's education, or science, or even English, has a respected place in most school programs, but little attention is given to educating youths in the primary responsibility most will have in life.

Tchudi: Communicating with the public is also a high priority on my list, but successful talk with the public involves a tightrope act: On the one hand, English teachers are the ones who *know* the field and its pedagogy and should make crucial decisions (including selection of books to be read); on the other hand, we need to respect the concerns and fears of parents, know their desires for their children, and incorporate these in our teaching. I think success in this area may come from improved public relations strategies, but this is also a curriculum matter. If English curricula were to become more strongly interdisciplinary and incorporate community-based or "real-world" learning activities, many public fears would be quieted.

McHugh: These fears are shown by the increase in censorship, which, combined with a determination to standardize and narrow the curriculum, forms a frightening and appalling trend. It is counter to the international/interrelational thrust of human relations. It is stunting the intellectual and social growth of students. In addition, media fixation is a reality and a problem for the growth of many skills we consider important to the development of *whole* human beings. The reduction of reading caused by television alone should be cause for concern. Since reading is a primary stimulus for learning ideas, developing the imagination, internalizing syntax, grammar, and mechanics, and extending vocabulary, its reduction leads to a retarding of young adult development and the potential atrophy of development in older adults. The relationship of impaired reading ability to impaired writing ability completes the process of tightening the circle of development and reducing the human potential to an ever-narrower area.

Question: How, then, can we expect to see change in the schools? What are the priorities for curricular reform?

Tchudi: The reform reports of the 1980s provide no real direction or, at best, false directions that point toward "back-to-basics." It is discouraging to note that after seventy-five years of campaigning for a more-or-less consistent set of language-learning principles, NCTE and its members have created only surface changes in the way English is taught in most schools. Is it possible to train a new generation of teachers in the principles of contemporary English instruction and hope that they will have impact? Is it desirable for NCTE and its members to fight for state or nationally mandated curricula based on sound English theory and practice? Or will new ideas continue to penetrate actual classrooms only by trickle-down and seep-through mechanisms? Without being evangelistic or inappropriately idealistic, I believe that we must look at the possibilities for widespread change, and make the discovery of new methods of effecting change a high priority.

McHugh: Humanities will surely become a prominent focus in the near future. NCTE can help to make this a multicultural, bihemispheric (in terms of the brain) focus rather than a 1950s focus (or worse!). Important questions include: How can an "integrated language arts" approach be designed and implemented K–12? How can music and art (and math and physics) be integrated experientially into English humanities curricula? The connections among computers, thinking skills, and problem solving might also be an interesting and important issue. Global education and English language arts have not yet come together very much or very frequently. They should.

Lloyd-Jones: The day of the department of English is almost over. We will soon have departments of American comprising American literature and language. Ethnic studies, film, women's studies, world literature, popular culture, various kinds of writing programs, thematic courses—all have undermined the base in English. In this context Shakespeare will become an American author—as he is a German author in their translated versions. Other authors will be read in part because important American writers were interested in them.

Such developments have already moved far in the schools and two-year colleges, and are edging into the four-year colleges, despite the perceptions of some scholars that all sense of taste has disappeared. A nation has a right—an obligation—to concentrate on the study of its own culture and language. In a pluralistic society that means we have to experience the language and literature of various subgroups as well as learn the features of several common dialects. We must study the best our nation has to offer, but that does not always mean the production of the most powerful or numerous.

Just as we need to know much about the variety of our own nation we have to be aware of the conceptions of other cultures. Although many take for granted the need to study "major" languages I mean to include here third-world literatures as well. One probably cannot sample all nations, but it is reasonable to pick a few for area study that includes literature.

Question: Are there other curriculum areas you'd like to see receive increased attention?

Fitzgerald: I have two others. Under pressure to have students master content, many parents, administrators, and teachers have lost sight of the prime goal of education: to develop the interests, habits, and abilities that will help students be *lifelong learners,* doubters, planners, and evaluators.

In addition, there is growing awareness of the significance of *listening and speaking skills* as foundations for all life roles, and current research is documenting the importance of oral language in the development of reading and writing. But few school programs reflect these understandings, and teacher education programs are woefully inadequate in preparing professionals who understand the importance and the methodologies of oral language instruction.

Tchudi: Textbooks are a major barrier to curriculum reform; we need better ones. There is nothing intrinsically evil about a textbook. Indeed, the textbook is a remarkably compact way of storing information. (Much is made of the compactness and capacity of a floppy computer disk, but one doesn't need a two-thousand-dollar electronic apparatus to read a book.) However, textbook production in this country has been complicated by mass merchandising and contemporary high-profit economic theory. The result is that the vast majority of mass-produced textbooks are conservative in nature and often dead wrong in their pedagogy. These books continue to control the English curriculum as manufacturers vigorously promote them and English teachers (who ought to know better) continue to buy them. Reform in this area can be achieved in a variety of ways. We have the know-how in this profession to teach without "texts," drawing on libraries to create an individualized reading program. However, English teachers also need to work actively to convey to publishers that we want better books, books that reflect current research and theory in English teaching. Then, when such books appear, we must educate colleagues to buy them.

Question: Are there areas of research that could help support curriculum reform?

McHugh: There are a number of unanswered questions where research can provide direction. Among them: Reading and writing—what is their interrelationship in light of recent and promising information on brain structure, holographic functioning, and learning processes? Class size—how can we (*can* we?) prove that class size makes a difference not only in teacher perception and performance but also in student perception and performance? Focus on the inner city (an 80 to 99 percent "minority" in ten major cities of the country)—what have we learned about the special needs of these children? What have we done to delight them with learning? What problems do we still have to solve? How can we interest (high school), train (college), and support (NCTE) new teachers of minorities (both minority teachers and teachers dedicated to teaching minorities) in English as a "way of life"?

Fitzgerald: Research must also be geared to help the classroom teacher. An aura of respectability surrounds research in K–12 education that is not granted to preparation for instruction in K–12 classrooms. This seems ironic because the ultimate purpose of all but a small portion of educational research is to affect instruction. It is also ironic because the methods and the data of such reports are couched in terms and numbers and tables that have little meaning for practitioners.

It seems to me that too many of the topics selected for research in education are unimportant given the problems practitioners face. In too many instances, the research outcomes are blatantly self-evident, without the research, to those who have adequate classroom teaching experience. Herein lies some of the answer: Nearly all researchers in elementary and secondary education should be expected to document their long-term, full-time, successful teaching in K–12 classrooms.

Question: What can NCTE do in coming years to address some of the problems you describe?

McHugh: For the past seventy-five years, the Council has broadened considerably in size, in focus, in multiplicity of services and considerations. It is to be commended for being able to preserve a core of commitment, stable policies for excellence, and forward thrust throughout such a long history. It is a prestigious organization. It may be faulted, understandably, however, for growing apace while its affiliates lag. The move toward hierarchy and bureaucracy is inexorable in American society—or has been in the last fifty years.

Lloyd-Jones: The Council is basically a confederation of sections, assemblies, conferences, and affiliates. We share convention dates—partly—and a headquarters staff. We sometimes agree on common awards and policies. But we are often driven by dissimilar imperatives, and we work under an astonishing variety of conditions. Although most of us teach, some of our subjects differ more from each other than they differ from those of widely various departments outside of English. The confederation allows us the numbers of people and income to undertake many major tasks, but it limits our common ground and tempts us to become preoccupied with *systems* of organization and with parceling out resources.

In the United States educational politics are essentially local despite national studies and federal initiatives—usually in research. Our affiliates have more useful political clout at the level of important educational actions than the Council as a whole does, but the Council can supply information and conduct research to make the affiliates effective. Both hands are required.

Fitzgerald: More help needs to be provided to affiliates so that they may become more influential on state and local levels. Affiliate development and their visibility in the national organization need to be priorities. Much of the direction, continuity, and understanding of core problems comes from the leadership NCTE Headquarters has provided over the years. The directorate and the efficient office personnel certainly are to be commended. We need to remind ourselves, however, that this is an organization of members and that the staff works with the members to promote the members' goals and aspirations for the organization and the profession.

Tchudi: We have to face the fact that the National Council of Teachers of English has become a bureaucracy. It is a humanistic bureaucracy, as opposed to a materialistic one, but it is a bureaucracy nonetheless. My greatest worry for the Council is that it will evolve into a kind of paper organization, continually passing rules, regulations, recommendations, and resolutions which have no impact on the teaching lives of its members or on the rest of the English teaching profession. We sometimes rejoice in the healthy diversity of NCTE and in its capability of tolerating divergent points of view. At the same time, the Council has lost some of the focus it had during its early years. No "task force" or "organizational reform" committee can solve this problem; indeed, the recommendations of such groups would probably just become another chapter in the organizational archives.

McHugh: The Council's most important task is to shift some of the burden for action, political and professional, to regional and local groups, with the Council providing support and impetus for grassroots development.

Fitzgerald: Only a small percentage of the elementary and secondary teachers who teach English language arts choose to attend, or have the chance to attend, our conferences. Not nearly enough read our journals and books. This is sad not only for them and for the children they teach; it also diminishes the effectiveness of our organization. We need to use our influence to see that K–12 teachers have released time and are encouraged to attend NCTE conferences and to offer sessions; that they are aware of our language arts publications and see the need to read them; and that classroom teachers hold positions of influence in affiliates and in the central bodies of the national organization.

Question: One final question—What is your vision of what school and college English might become in the next twenty-five years, by the time NCTE celebrates its centennial? Do you have some outlandish ideas or visions for the profession?

McHugh: "Inner-city" conferences. International conferences that include many nations beyond traditional "English-speaking" countries. The use of public schools (all levels) for ongoing education and interactive experiments (all age groups, eight to eighty). Computer education, multicultural experiences, humanities, "Foxfire"-type local programs onsite in schools.

Outreach programs involving promising high school students. The establishment of a retired teachers' assembly. The design and implementation of a research program based on interaction between local universities and elementary and secondary schools. Teachers and researchers working together in the classroom—hypothesizing, designing research, conducting research, writing it up, presenting it.

Tchudi: English (or language) truly is *the* central discipline in learning. Yet for most of this century, English classes have dwelt on but a small surface of the universe of discourse: namely traditional (not excluding contemporary) literature and a few writing genres. My vision for 2011 is that English teachers will dramatically extend the "definition" of English by expanding the kinds of reading, writing, speaking, and listening that children do. In broad theory, there is no need for English as a separate discipline because it encompasses all disciplines; in practice, a broadly interdisciplinary English program, a multiple-literacy program, can be the heart of every child's schooling by NCTE's centennial.

McHugh: NCTE should be committed to communication on an international level. At the present, and presumably for some time in the future, English is the "lingua franca" for diplomacy, science, business, and cultural exchange. Teaching proficiency and sufficiency is a commitment. Teachers want their students at all levels to appreciate the richness and variety of language (in this case English), to be able to understand and produce basic communication, to infer nuance, and to increase the possibility of true exchange of ideas and feelings. This competency and versatility holds the promise, obviously idealistic but nonetheless desirable, that one day peoples of this earth will be able to hear and respond to each other with dignity, respect, and brother/sisterhood, and then be able to translate words into action. Prejudice is primarily the result of ignorance and miscommunication. Instruction in English as a tool for communication on all levels, from the mundane to the most metaphoric, is a key and tool for internal and international understanding.

The View from Headquarters

John C. Maxwell

One of the perpetual and ultimately unanswerable questions is: What is NCTE? To some who think in terms of mortar and brick, the Headquarters is the Council. But of course it is not. The Council is out there, among the members, as an intangible ideal, arising from the simple notion, expressed before our founding in 1911: that there ought to be "a national council of teachers of English." And so it came to be.

Even ideals and ideas must be shaped, stored, sent and received, accounted for, and tended by caring hands. And so we have a headquarters building of some 30,000 square feet; a staff of more than eighty persons; computers, printing presses, telephones, lights, and walls; and carpeting which, though frayed in spots, is still serviceable after fifteen years. It is, though, but a house which the family of English teachers regards as their home. At least for now.

The major issue before the staff of the Council is how best to give concrete form to ideas and make those materials available as readily and economically as possible to teachers and scholars. A subsidiary purpose is to provide financial stability and strength for both the present and the future. The means by which these purposes are fulfilled is our sense of service and our ability to fulfill the needs of teachers, both those who are members and those who are not. In this regard, a central issue is sometimes how to locate and provide information useful to teachers when they need to know about a curriculum problem, a growing trend, a disputed theory. In this regard, Headquarters often serves as a "switching point," which can put questioners into contact with other people who have answers.

The persisting, pervading questions of the profession, as outlined in the chapters of this book, provide for headquarters staff a framework for thinking about the needs of the profession and what we can do to provide resources for those who want to pursue these issues. Through our archives and our collective memory we can sometimes save an investigator the trouble of searching for something that has already been found, or perhaps help by putting the topic into some sort of historical perspective.

Thus some of the headquarters resources form the "memory" of the Council and the profession.

One of the most unnerving phrases we hear is "NCTE says . . ." Those who use it may refer to an article in a journal, a chapter in a book, or—worse yet—a chance utterance from somebody at Headquarters. The phrase suggests an authority and a finality that are unwarranted. There is a tendency to believe we have the answers here, and, true, we have some. But English language arts is a field in which there are few irrefutable answers. Even when research has appeared to point toward some firm directions or truths, there still is Sophocles' nagging question, "What if it's otherwise?"

We must perceive the Council as a continuing forum for the exploration of possible truths about the art and science of teaching English. The task of the headquarters staff is to sustain that open forum through both print and oral, and occasionally visual, means. The direction and shape of the debate within the forum is determined by the larger membership and, particularly, those who voice the varieties of possible truths and those who determine the policies that guide the professional staff in their work. Our hope is that by our work that search will be expressed in useful forms of high quality.

Afterword

The Dialogue Continues . . .

> "A word is dead when it is said, some say. I say it just begins to live that day."
>
> —Emily Dickinson

This yearbook reports a part of the conversation that began on December 1 and 2, 1911, at Chicago's Great Northern Hotel, when a small group of English teachers drafted the charter of a Council that was, in the words of J. N. Hook, "born of protest [against the rigidity of a university-determined curriculum] but inspired by altruistic urges"[1] (to give *all* students, not just the college-bound, the power to read and to use language effectively). Hook adds the information that this conversation was limited in 1911 to a small circle of mainly Anglo-Saxon-surnamed high school and college teachers. As George Henry wrote in 1984, much of the Council's continuing dialogue was informed by this same "inherent dialectic between tradition and reform."[2]

Charlotte Brooks pointed in 1985 to a second dialectic that marks our expanding circle—the newer dynamic of open communication among our varied traditions and cultures: To teach well students whose life-experience is different from the Anglo-Saxon/American traditions, we need first to acquire "a clear, true, and informed view of [their] own language, literature, and culture."[3]

In 1986 the whole profession of education is on notice that "by the year 2000, one out of every three Americans will be a member of a minority group"[4] . . . black, Hispanic, Asian, or Native American. And NCTE president Richard Lloyd-Jones, in his inaugural remarks, restated thus the dialogic nature of all our learning and teaching—across the impulses to tradition and to reform, across the distinctions of our ethnic, cultural differences: "We know ourselves better when we discover others."

What follows is a list of Council members from the whole range of our constantly growing conversational circle who have participated—along with chapter authors and members of the Yearbook Committee—in the dialogue that shaped this yearbook. Their contributions, written and spoken, included advice, correction, encouragement, criticism, commentary.

Our conversations took place by mail and phone; in meetings, hotel lobbies, airports—wherever English teachers exchange ideas and inform and learn from one another. Their advice was always appreciated, always influential, sometimes followed. The editor of this yearbook and all its readers—all who will continue the dialogue—say a most hearty and sincere *thanks* to each and to all!

Correspondents, conversationalists, critics, encouragers, advisors include. . . .

Nicholas Alexander, Abington, PA
Virginia French Allen, Boulder, CO
Arthur Applebee, Stanford, CA
Bruce Appleby, Carbondale, IL
Richard W. Bailey, Ann Arbor, MI
James Brewbaker, Columbus, GA
Jackie Bryant, Virginia Beach, VA
Carlota Cardeñas de Dwyer, San Antonio, TX
Martha Cobb, Washington, DC
Merron Chorny, Calgary, Alberta, Canada
Mary Coleman, Drexel Hill, PA
Paul Crowley, Columbia, MO
James Davis, Cedar Rapids, IA
Deborah De Zure, Ann Arbor, MI
Lahna Diskin, Trenton, NJ
Janet Evans, West Islip, NY
Edmund Farrell, Austin, TX
Jacqueline Brice Finch, St. Croix, VI
Elizabeth Foster, N. Chelmsford, MA
Kris Gutierrez, Boulder, CO
Rose Glassberg, Glassboro, NJ
Roseann Gonzalez, Tucson, AZ
Kenneth Goodman, Tucson, AZ
Yetta Goodman, Tucson, AZ
Jerome Green, New York, NY
Lolita Rose Green, Chicago, IL
Arnold Griese, Fairbanks, AK
Alfred Grommon, Portola Valley, CA
Shirley Haley-James, Marietta, GA
Richard Hanzelka, Davenport, IA
Nan Harden, San Antonio, TX
Julia Higgs, Huntington Station, NY
Patricia House, Virginia Beach, VA
Janice Hull, Southfield, MI
Dell Hymes, Philadelphia, PA

Jay Jacoby, Charlotte, NC
Joan Kinney, Bedford, MA
Carol Kuykendall, Houston, TX
Marguerite R. Lyle, Lafayette, LA
Barrett Mandel, New Brunswick, NJ
David Munson-Young, Billings, MT
Kathleen Morner, Oak Park, IL
Carol A. Pope, Houston, TX
Miles Myers, Oakland, CA
Gordon Pradl, New York, NY
Robert Probst, Atlanta, GA
Corinne Procope, Yeadon, PA
Alan Purves, Melrose, NY
Mary Ella Randall, Silver Spring, MD
Paula Mia Rollins, Albany, NY
Edgar H. Schuster, Allentown, PA
Ellen Shull, San Antonio, TX
Geneva Smitherman, Detroit, MI
Margaret Stevenson, Edmonton, Alberta, Canada
Lois Stover, Springfield, OH
Dorothy Strickland, New York, NY
C. James Trotman, West Chester, PA
Darwin Turner, Iowa City, IA
Edwyna Wheadon, Houston, TX
Velez Wilson, New Orleans, LA
Seymour Yesner, Brookline, MA
Jane Zaharias, Cleveland, OH
Richard Zahner, Stratford, CT

. . . many others—and you.

Marjorie N. Farmer
Philadelphia, PA

Notes

1. J. N. Hook, *A Long Way Together: A Personal View of NCTE's First Sixty-Seven Years* (Urbana, Ill.: National Council of Teachers of English, 1979), 3.
2. George H. Henry, "The Council: How Shall It Survive?" *College English* 46, no. 7 (Nov. 1984): 668.
3. Charlotte Brooks, ed., *Tapping Potential: English and Language Arts for the Black Learner* (Urbana, Ill.: National Council of Teachers of English, 1985), 6.
4. Carnegie Forum on Education and the Economy, *A Nation Prepared: Teachers for the Twenty-First Century,* Report of the Task Force on Teaching as a Profession (New York: Carnegie Forum on Education and the Economy, 1986), 14.

Contributors

Harold B. Allen is professor emeritus of English and linguistics at the University of Minnesota, and has served as director of the Commission on the English Language, president of the American Dialect Society, and president of the National Council of Teachers of English. His books include *The Teaching of English to Non-English Speakers, Pathways to English,* and *Regional Dialects, 1945–1974.*

Rexford Brown is director of communications and a senior policy analyst for the Education Commission of the States. He is the former director of publications for the National Assessment of Educational Progress, chair of the NCTE Standing Committee on Testing and Evaluation, and the author, coauthor, or editor of numerous reports, books, articles, and policy studies on testing and education, including *Reading, Thinking, and Writing, Art and Young Americans,* and *Writing Achievement, 1969–1979.*

Paul T. Bryant is dean of the graduate college and professor of English at Radford University. He is a founding editor of the *Journal of English Teaching Techniques,* a former director of the NCTE Commission on Composition, and a former president of the College English Association. His publications include a book on H. L. Davis, short stories, and poems, as well as articles in *Connections, College Composition and Communication,* and the *CEA Critic.*

Miriam T. Chaplin is associate professor of education at Rutgers University and a visiting scholar for the National Assessment of Educational Progress at the Educational Testing Service. Formerly vice president of the NCTE Black Caucus, she is currently a member of the NCTE Executive Committee and incoming chair of the Conference on College Composition and Communication. She is the author of *Reading Comes to College* and a contributor to *Tapping Potential: English and Language Arts for the Black Learner* (ed. Charlotte Brooks), as well as journals such as the *Journal of Reading, English Education,* and *Education Digest.*

Ouida Clapp is director emeritus of the language arts program in the Buffalo, New York, Public Schools, current cochair of the NCTE Committee on American Literature and the American Multicultural Heritage, and former president of the New York State English Council. She is coauthor of *Patterns in Literature,* editor of three volumes of the NCTE Classroom Practices in Teaching English series, and a contributor to *Three Language-Arts Curriculum Models: Pre-Kindergarten through College.* In 1986 the National Association for the Advancement of Colored People presented her with its Medgar Evers Award.

Marjorie Nichols Farmer is executive director emeritus of the English/reading curriculum for the School District of Philadelphia and an educational consultant to the U.S. Department of Education, the Educational Testing Service, and others. A former president of the National Council of Teachers of English, she is the author of *Career Education and the Teaching of English* and (with others) of the Laidlaw English Series.

Sheila Fitzgerald is a professor in the Department of Teacher Education at Michigan State University. She is a past president of both the Michigan Council of Teachers of English and the National Council of Teachers of English and has given numerous presentations here and abroad on the elementary language arts, including reading instruction, poetry for children, talking and listening skills, and education in an international perspective.

Allan Glatthorn is a professor of education in the Graduate School of Education at the University of Pennsylvania, chair of the Curriculum Advisory Council of the National Association of Secondary School Principals, and chair of the Publications Committee of the Association for Supervision and Curriculum Development. His books include *Curriculum Leadership, Writing for Success,* and *Differentiated Supervision.*

Catherine C. Hatala is director of the reading/English language arts program for the School District of Philadelphia and president of the Pennsylvania Council of Secondary School English Department Chairmen. She has been a frequent speaker at state and national conferences on writing to learn, teaching writing to the special education student, and the reading/mathematics connection.

Theodore Hipple is head of the Department of Curriculum and Instruction at the University of Tennessee, a member of the NCTE Executive Committee, and current chair of the NCTE Secondary Section Committee. His publications include *Successful Business English* and *Teaching English in Secondary Schools,* as well as over seventy articles in such journals as *English Journal, English Education,* and *Phi Delta Kappan.*

Richard Lloyd-Jones is a professor of English and department chair at the University of Iowa at Iowa City and 1985–86 president of the National Council of Teachers of English. A former chair of the Conference on College Composition and Communication and member of NCTE's Editorial Board, he is the author of *Research in Written Composition* (with Richard Braddock and Lowell Schoer) and *Technical and Scientific Writing* (with C. Andrews).

John C. Maxwell has been executive director of the National Council of Teachers of English since 1981, after serving as Deputy Executive Director for National Relations from 1977–81 and Associate Executive Secretary from 1971–77. Previously he had been a high school teacher and K–12 supervisor in cities in Nebraska, Wisconsin, and Minnesota. He has served NCTE as director of the Commission on English Curriculum, chair of the Secondary Section Committee, member of the Committee on Publications, and member of the NCTE Executive Committee. His publications include *Backgrounds in Language, On Writing Behavioral Objectives for English* (with Anthony Tovatt), and articles in *English Journal, NEA Journal, Publishers Weekly,* and *Education Week.*

Nancy S. McHugh is a teacher of English to grades 10 through 12 at Grant High School in Van Nuys, California, and president elect of the National Council of Teachers of English. She has served as chair of the NCTE Committee on Exceptional Children, chair of the NCTE Nominating Committee, and chair of the Secondary Section Nominating Committee, as well as NCTE's representative to the National Testing/Evaluation Conference. She is the author of several publications on writing for the Los Angeles Unified School District and has been a leader or speaker for numerous workshops and sessions around the country.

Beatrice S. Moore is adjunct professor of literature and composition at St. Joseph's University in Philadelphia and vice president of the Delaware Valley Writing Council. She has published articles in *Educational Perspectives* and the *DVWC Newsletter,* as well as *Notes on Teaching English* for the Georgia-South Carolina English Association.

Ben F. Nelms is professor of English education at the University of Missouri, director of the Missouri Writing Project, and a member of the advisory committee to the National Writing Project. A former editor of *English Education,* current chair of the NCTE Yearbook Committee, and incoming editor of *English Journal,* he is the author of articles on young adult literature, the teaching of writing, and English education in such journals as *English Education,* the *Missouri English Bulletin,* and *English Journal,* as well as a chapter in *Literature for Adolescents.*

P. A. Ramsey is examiner in test development and coordinator in the Visiting Scholar Program for the higher education program of the Educational Testing Service in Princeton, New Jersey. A former assistant professor of English at the State University of New York at Binghamton, he was the organizer and codirector of the Writing Center on that campus. He is the editor of *Rome in the Renaissance: The City and the Myth,* and has given numerous presentations around the country on writing, Afro-American literature, and testing.

Donald L. Rubin is jointly appointed as associate professor in the departments of Speech Communication and Language Education at the University of Georgia, where he is also a fellow in the Institute for Behavioral Research. A member of the NCTE Standing Committee on Research and the Committee on Professional Writing Networks for Teachers and Supervisors, Rubin has contributed chapters to such books as *Exploring Speaking-Writing Relationships: Connections and Contrasts* and *Speaking and Writing K–12: Classroom Strategies and the New Research,* and his articles have appeared in *Research in the Teaching of English, Communication Education, Written Communication,* and *Child Development.*

Rudine Sims is a professor in the Department of Educational Theory and Practice at the Ohio State University. She has served as chair of the NCTE Elementary Section, chair of the NCTE Committee on Resolutions, and national program chair of the National Conference on the Teaching of Language Arts in the Elementary

School. Her contributions to the field include chapters in *What's New in Reading?* (ed. Iris Tiedt), *Findings of Research in Reading Miscue Analysis: Classroom Implications* (ed. P. David Allen and Dorothy J. Watson), and *Reader Meets Author/Bridging the Gap: A Psycholinguistic and Sociolinguistic Perspective* (ed. Judith Langer and Margaret Smith-Burke), as well as numerous presentations at conventions of the National Council of Teachers of English and the International Reading Association, among others.

James R. Squire is senior vice president emeritus at Ginn and Company Publishers in Boston. He was executive secretary of the National Council of Teachers of English from 1960–67, chair of the NCTE Task Force on Excellence in English, director of the National Study of High School English Programs, director of the Study of High School English Programs in the United Kingdom, member of the steering committee of the Anglo-American Seminar on the Teaching of English and president of the National Conference on Research in English. He is the author of *Teaching Language and Literature* (with Walter Loban and Margaret Ryan), *The National Interest and the Teaching of English* (with the Committee on National Interest), and *High School English Instruction Today: The National Study of High School English Programs* (with Roger K. Applebee), as well as over one hundred articles in such journals as *English Journal, College English, PMLA,* and the *NEA Journal.*

Charles Suhor is deputy executive director of the National Council of Teachers of English and director of the ERIC Clearinghouse on Reading and Communication Skills. While teaching English and serving as English supervisor for the New Orleans Public Schools he was active as an NCTE affiliate president and as a member of various Council groups, including the Commission on the English Curriculum and the SLATE Steering Committee. His interest in media and semiotics is reflected in numerous writings for *Educational Leadership, Educational Researcher, English Journal, Et Cetera, Journal of Curriculum Studies, Media and Methods,* and others. He edited (with Christopher Thaiss) *Speaking and Writing K–12: Classroom Strategies and the New Research,* and is currently collaborating on a book about teaching concrete poetry.

Stephen N. Tchudi is a professor of English at Michigan State University and currently a visiting professor at the University of Sydney in Australia. He has served as president of the National Council of Teachers of English as well as chair of the Secondary Section and member of the Executive Committee of the Conference on English Education. He is also a past president of the Michigan Council of Teachers of English and recipient of its Charles Carpenter Fries Award for service to the profession. His publications include *The ABCs of Literacy, Writing in Reality* (with James Miller), *An English Teacher's Handbook* (with Susan Tchudi), and *Explorations in the Teaching of English;* articles in such journals as *Media and Methods, English Education, English Journal,* and *College Composition and Communication;* and a novel for young adults, *The Burg-O-Rama Man.*